SEIZE
THE · DAY

Your Church Can Survive. Thrive!

Rev. John J. Rogers
Church of Christ
in christian union

SEIZE

THE · DAY

Your Church
Can
Su~~rvive.~~
Thrive!

by H.C. Wilson

Foreword by John C. Maxwell

DEDICATION

At the time of his death in 1955, a fellow pastor penned these words that were shared at his funeral:

He was, in my estimation, a magnanimous man, a man with a great soul. He was big enough to rejoice in another's success and to weep at another's loss; to encourage the disheartened and the inexperienced; to be kind to everyone and to be thoughtful of the needy; to take note of the children and to remember the aged; to support his leaders on the one hand and to serve his people on the other; to live for Christ and to forget himself. He indeed was and is an overcomer. He has joined the cloud of witnesses who cheer us on. I see his beaming smile and twinkling eyes, his characteristic upraised hand of greeting, and the race becomes easier, the distance shorter, and the prospect more glorious.

FOREWORD

Church growth books can have a limiting affect upon church leaders. Their description of the "ideal" pastor or environment to grow a congregation can be depressing. Few church leaders possess the abilities that these books seem to require. Fewer still have the ideal church setting that seems conducive for growth. The result? Frustration.

Dr. Wilson's book has a different approach. Its emphasis is not so much on the location of the church, but on the leadership of the pastor. It recognizes the spirit of the leader is more important than the sociological factors of the church. My own spirit soared each time I read the words at the close of each chapter: *"It is not a matter of gifts or talents, location or population base. It's a matter of the heart. Carpe Diem—SEIZE THE DAY!"*

This book draws the picture of a healthy, balanced congregation. The words were written by a man who sees the church through the eyes of a successful pastor and church leader . . . the eyes of experience and maturity. For the young pastor, this book will serve as a blueprint for future ministry. For the middle-aged pastor, this book will serve as a checklist for present ministry.

As you read this book, get ready to do the following things: (1) Take note of and file away many practical principles and illustrations. (2) Stop and reflect on the balance of your present ministry. (3) Pray and commit yourself to lead a thriving church.

Remember, *"It is not a matter of gifts or talents, location or population base. It's a matter of the heart."* Read this book and *SEIZE THE DAY!*

Dr. John C. Maxwell
Senior Pastor
Skyline Wesleyan Church
Lemon Grove, California

ACKNOWLEDGMENTS

The completion of any book is a cooperative effort and this one is no exception. To many I owe genuine gratitude and appreciation:

— to the pastors and people in many churches of varying sizes in very diverse circumstances where I have had the privilege to observe thriving ministry that helped to stimulate the thrust of this book,

— to a number of my ministerial colleagues for the frequent nudging to put these thoughts in writing,

— to my wife, Gloria, and our children who have been a constant source of encouragement and support to me in this project,

— to my secretary, Debra Levite, for her excellent work in the several rewrites of this material,

— to God who paid a debt He did not owe, I owe a debt I cannot pay.

CONTENTS

A THRIVING CHURCH WILL . . .

INTRODUCTION

DIED ... SURVIVED ... THRIVED ... One of these words will, with accuracy, describe every church in our nation as we stand in just a few short years at the dawning of a new decade, a new century and a new millennium. As we hesitate momentarily at that historic threshold and gaze back over the landscape of the '90s, we may well see that 10-15 percent of all evangelical churches in America have died, 70-80 percent have survived and 10-15 percent have truly thrived. These are poignant days for the church as we stand in the shadow of the year 2000 sensing its magnetic pull.

2000. A year that has long held significance to the church. A year that some have felt would be a turning time for all of history. It is a time of questions, uncertainties and speculation. The end of time? Will the Temple be rebuilt? Armageddon? Rapture? Tribulation? Are you pre-, post- or mid-? While I would not for a moment want to suggest that such discussion is out of order it may well be that the preoccupation with these topics in some circles is a diversionary tactic of the enemy. Keep the focus on things that cannot be proven and stir endless debate while real ministry is sidelined.

Operation Desert Shield and Operation Desert Storm helped to bring on a new surge of books on prophecy and end-time matters. The swirling currents of Middle East events is made even more compelling by the looming shadow of A.D. 2000.

Before we run off to draw a new prophecy chart focused on 2000, we must give ourselves to ministry now. What 2000 holds is known only to God. But we have this moment for ministry. A moment for which we will be held accountable. The crucial question is not what will happen in 2000. The truly crucial question is what will we do with the responsibility clearly before us in the '90s.

Every generation and every decade is a matter of history—an historical fact. Only a few generations and a few decades, in addition to being historical realities, have also been historic because of their contributions to mankind or because they occupied some pivot point in the time line of humanity.

For decade upon decade and even for centuries in some slices of time, nothing of historic consequence seems to have taken place. We remember that in 1492 Columbus sailed the ocean blue but what about the 1330s or the 1120s or the 1550s or the silent years of the Dark Ages? Decades come and go and come and go.

> *The crucial question is not what will happen in 2000. The truly crucial question is what will we do with the responsibility clearly before us in the '90s.*

But not this one. We are truly in an historic time capsule identified as the 1990s. We will, in a few years, enter not only a new decade and a new century but also a new millennium. None of us have ever experienced such a time previously. None of us will ever experience such a time in the future. What a time this is!

This is the point in time that Alvin Toffler referred to as "the hinge of history." Our place in history is thrust upon us by more than just the calender. We are in a decade of unprecedented change in our society and in our world.

In preparation for the writing of their book *The Day America Told the Truth*, the authors confidentially interviewed hundreds of people in all regions of the United States. They rather arbitrarily divided the U.S. into six regions and intensely interviewed people in each of these regions. The purpose of the regional approach was to allow for local, area or sectional slant or bias in the responses to the questions posed. Even with regional differences of opinion and values taken into consideration, several common threads were found woven into the American life-fabric all across the country.

Their research led them to some startling conclusions:

There is absolutely no moral consensus at all in the 1990s. Here are extraordinary new commandments for the 1990s:

1. I don't see the point in observing the Sabbath.
2. I will steal from those who won't really miss it.
3. I will lie when it suits me, so long as it doesn't cause any real damage.
4. I will drink and drive if I feel I can handle it. I know my limit.
5. I will cheat on my spouse—after all, given the chance, he or she will do the same.
6. I will procrastinate at work and do absolutely nothing about one full day in every five. It's

standard operating procedure.
7.   I will use recreational drugs.
8.   I will cheat on my taxes—to a point. [1]

In the book of Judges we read "Every man did that which was right in his own eyes." This descriptive statement of a long past generation also seems to fit our generation. What a time this is!

According to statistics released by Ted Engstrom of World Vision, Islam is growing by 16 percent per year, Buddhism by 10 percent and Christianity by 9 percent. There are now more Muslims than Baptists in Britain. What a time this is!

We now live in an information era. Our world is increasingly divided not between the "haves" and "have nots," but between the "knows" and "know nots." We are told that the *Encyclopedia Britannica* can be sent across the Atlantic six times a minute. If the auto industry had kept pace with the computer information advance, a Rolls Royce would get three million miles a gallon, would cost less than $3 and you could put six on the head of a pin. What a time this is!

It was reported by the media that Governor Mario Cuomo of New York gave a speech at the University of Notre Dame in which he addressed the abortion issue. He was quoted as saying that as a Catholic he believed abortion was wrong and that the teaching of his church was right, but as long as the majority of the citizens of his state did not favor that position, he was not morally obligated to carry it out.

Positions based on popularity rather than principle. What a time this is!

It was reported recently that the Russian parliament went into recess for the express purpose of allowing the members to receive free Bibles that were being distributed in the halls outside the legislative chambers. In more than one former communist country in Eastern Europe, the Bible is used as a textbook for the teaching of the English language. According to the *National and International Religion Report* Soviet education officials have approved a moral education project. The project reportedly will include the establishment of three pilot schools in Moscow where moral values will be taught from a Christian perspective.

Meanwhile, in "one nation under God" the seemingly relentless determination by forces of influence to purge the society of any reference to the divine continues apace. The United States seems to be sliding down a slippery slope leading to a psyche in society that is anti-God and increasingly belligerent toward religion, especially the conservative, evangelical brand with its message of sin and salvation and clean living expectations. What a time this is!

Joe Ellis, in his book, *The Church on Purpose* said,

> It is also a time of opportunity. When foundations are shaken, doors often fly open unexpectedly. Our time has been described as the greatest opportunity for the church in this century.[2]

History repeats itself again as we stand astride a moment in God's time-line that is truly the best of times and the worst of times. What a time this is!

The present decade is already unfolding before us as a period of unprecedented change in our culture and in our churches. To borrow a line from Youth for Christ history, the need to be *Anchored to the Rock and Geared to the Times* will be important to the point of determining first survival and then viability in ministry.

> History repeats itself again as we stand astride a moment in God's time-line that is truly the best of times and the worst of times.

DIED

Some churches because they were *Anchored to the Rock and Geared to the Past* will cease to exist and go to their grave with the mistaken belief that they were defending the truth in a hopeless environment. They may well have been theologically sound but their demise will have resulted from their rigid and timeworn methodology coupled with a corporate paranoia over change.

They will pass from the scene while stoutly defending the unnecessary. Still fighting the Battle of Bunker Hill. Having fallen into the deadly trap of mistaking inflexibility for spirituality, some will move into extinct status actually feeling a bit proud of the fact that they refused to "compromise."

Others will expire that were *Anchored to the Times and Geared to the Times.* Having fallen prey to the equally deadly urge to follow every fad in the name of innovative ministry, some churches will exhaust themselves in the endless pursuit of the "leading edge" and cease operations. Their fatal flaw, the worship of methodology, will see change as an end in itself and they will march to the graveyard oblivious to the cause of their death.

Intoxicated with the false hope of cutting-edge

ministry, such churches will mistake style for substance, innovation for inspiration and activity for progress. The preparation for ministry of the parson or the people will be sacrificed on the altar of the latest program. All new and flashy videos, books and programs are purchased sight unseen in this driven church. Infected with "fad-itis," the patient tends to worsen as the disease feeds on itself and in extreme cases will lead to the demise of the church.

Helen Keller was once asked if there was anything she could think of worse than being blind. She answered, "Yes, being able to see and having no vision." This Keller axiom is the killer attitude of dying churches.

SURVIVED

The majority of churches will be in this group. They will have avoided the death rattle but will have failed to rise to the exhilarating but frightening challenges of relevant ministry. They will wring their hands, not ring the bell.

They will be involved in ongoing programs and will possess resources of people and money sufficient to keep them in operation. They will approach change with a combination of fear and suspicion on the one hand and hope and mild desperation on the other. They will even attempt certain innovations in ministry, but will not truly be a thriving unit.

Many good churches will be in this category. Their ministry will be respectable. Their buildings will be well kept and adequate. Their programs will be of acceptable quality. While facing little possibility of extinction they will also evidence little passion for excellence.

Many of these surviving churches will possess traits of the thriving unit. They will occasionally brush against greatness in ministry but will never quite break away from the pull of their safety net. The vast majority of churches will be in this group, perhaps as many as 80 percent. They will be *Anchored to the Rock and Almost Geared to the Times.*

THRIVED

Truly *Anchored to the Rock and Geared to the Times* these churches will balance a soundly biblical belief base with a thoroughly need-oriented methodology. Such churches will be located at country crossroads, in small towns and in massive cities. The impact of the thriving church will be determined largely by attitudes, approaches to ministry and spiritual priorities, and not primarily by location or population base.

The conditions that set the foundation for a thriving church are matters of the heart. They are attitudinal and philosophical. While methodology plays a vital role, the real battlefield in moving toward becoming a thriving church is a battle in the mind and in the heart. Thriving churches begin with the will to thrive.

In 1 Chronicles 12:32 we read a powerful statement concerning the descendents of Issachar ". . . the sons of Issachar had understanding of the times to know what Israel ought to do." Such a statement will accurately describe the thriving churches of this dynamic decade and into the 21st century, should the Master tarry.

The direction of this book is based on a variety of presuppositions, namely, that the pastors and people who read these pages are orthodox in their theology, converted in their hearts, sensitive in their spirits and world-class Christians in the making. There will be no attempt here to defend or explain the cardinal tenets of historic Christianity. These are accepted as givens.

This, then, is a book directed to the hearts and minds of all of us who share a common passion to be a part of a thriving church. It is not a matter of gifts or talents, location or population base. It's a matter of the heart. Carpe Diem—*SEIZE THE DAY!*

CHAPTER ONE

A Thriving Church Will . . .

AVOID THE FREQUENT FLYER SYNDROME

Most worshiping congregations drift into a period of passivity at one or more points in their life cycle.[3]

—Lyle Schaller

Religion is always in danger of substituting the dead letter for the life-giving spirit, of confidence in creed and ritual rather than in the power of the living God. The experience is as near as the next worship service in our own local church.[4]

—Bruce Shelley

"... keep your spiritual fervor" Romans 12:11.

A first-time airline passenger is easily identified by the frequent flyer while getting settled in the airplane prior to departure. The first-timer has an air of nervous excitement while facing this new and hopefully exhilarating experience. Common traits of the first-timer include not being sure where to sit, not understanding the routine procedures, not knowing where the restrooms are located, not knowing how long the flight will last and being uncertain whether or not to engage the person in the next seat in conversation.

While the first-timer is trying to cope with all the adjustments mentioned, the flight attendant begins the standard safety instruction explanation. Flotation devices are identified and their function explained; the location and activation of oxygen devices in the event of cabin depressurization are demonstrated; the locations of emergency exits are pointed out; the floor level emergency lighting color pattern is indicated; the safety feature explanation card is displayed for further reference.

The first-timer listens with rapt attention to every word given by the flight attendant. Eyes are glued to the presentation and ears and mind are straining together to absorb and assimilate the barrage of information. This is, after all, instruction designed to save the traveler's life.

Meanwhile, the frequent flyer is reading the newspaper or the current best-seller, or engaging in conversation with a companion, or gazing out the window as the mind daydreams, or perhaps even sleeping. In spite of the fact that the instructions of the flight attendant are designed to save lives, the frequent flyer is so accustomed to the routine and so aware of what will happen next that no need is recognized to pay attention and certainly no acknowledgment that what is going on might have real personal application. As the threadbare idiom puts it, familiarity breeds contempt.

Thriving churches will have first-timers as a rather regular experience. The joy of new birth, not just the artificial happiness from transfer growth, will mark the thriving church. Conversion builds the kingdom, transfer growth merely builds the church. Thriving churches will most certainly receive members by transfer. The warm and vibrant ministry of a thriving church will attract to the fellowship many from other churches where biblical belief has been sacrificed to the fool's gold proposition that compromise of principle is necessary for contemporary ministry. But conversion growth will be one of the common denominators and primary objectives of thriving churches.

> *The joy of new birth, not just the artificial happiness from transfer growth, will mark the thriving church.*

The pastor will stand before the congregation to give instruction and teaching designed to really save our lives. The lofty themes of the Trinity, atonement, redemption, forgiveness, salvation, eternity, judgment, the Holy Spirit's person and ministry, the church, the sacraments and the second coming will be dealt with periodically. These will be augmented by preaching/teaching on the practics of Christian living and the joy of service to Christ and the body.

The first-timer, searching for reality, will listen with

rapt attention and seek to understand the truth and then to identify means to apply the truth to life. To absorb and assimilate the barrage of information will stretch the new believer. The members of the family of faith who are in daily communication with the Master will be a real cheering section to these first-time flyers.

Watch out for the frequent attender syndrome. While things of eternal significance and their practical application are being taught, preached and discussed, the frequent attender may read the Sunday school paper, or engage in conversation with a companion on the pew, or gaze out the window as the mind daydreams, or in extreme cases perhaps even sleep. Churches may survive with the frequent attender syndrome; they cannot thrive when infected with this low-grade fever.

When I was attending elementary school in Nova Scotia, our school took part in a campaign to sell magazines in our community. We were all arbitrarily assigned a number of homes to visit for sales and sent out like lambs to the slaughter. I was not motivated. I was not enthused. I made my visits out of grim determination to get finished. Guilt and negative motivation drove me to participate.

I developed a fool-proof method to guarantee quick visits and no sales. My presentation went something like this: "Hello, we are selling magazines from the school. You don't want to buy any do you?" My presentation was pathetic. I was apathetic. While I could not have identified it as such at the time, I was displaying symptoms of the frequent flyer syndrome. No motivation. No enthusiasm. Guilt-ridden performance. Apathy.

In his book *How To Be A World Class Christian*, Paul Borthwick says,

Mission leaders, predicting the ability of the church to complete the Great Commission by the year 2000, list the local church as a major obstacle. Richard Solls of New Tribes Mission states, "By insufficient vision, discipleship, and obedience, the church has bottlenecked the flow of personnel and resources needed to do the job." Jim Reapsome of The Evangelical Missions Information Service adds, "In a nutshell, apathetic Christians are the biggest hurdle to overcome."[5]

Frequent flyer syndrome.

I was there not long ago. The building is quite adequate. The location is good. The population base is strong. The pastoral family is of better than average quality. But the vision has dimmed. A fortress mentality has set in. *We can advance* has been replaced with *we must hold on.* Church is becoming a chore to take care of rather than a joy to anticipate. No open sin here. No major church fight. The frequent flyer syndrome has set in. The gusto is gone.

Many times the momentum can be regained in such places. Not always, but often. Never without purposeful effort. Regrettably, too often the frequent flyer syndrome makes a frequent flyer out of the pastor. Sometimes necessary but often premature. A move to a new place and a new pastor for the old place. Revolving preachers. The temporary fix. The issues are not addressed and after the honeymoon is over, there it is again. Enemies are never conquered by retreat or surrender. They are conquered by superior strength and strategy in a face-to-face encounter. Such are at our disposal if we are controlled by the Christ and not the circumstance.

The gusto with which first generation people so fully give themselves to the task at hand is well known. Many are the examples of churches and mission or para-church organizations whose most explosive growth was during their first generation of existence. Driven by the vision of the founding fathers and their followers, many in reality did wondrous exploits for the Lord.

In succeeding generations the organizations often continue while the passion and vision of the founding first generation seems to lose intensity and is replaced by solid administration, good programming and fine facilities. We are told that at the time Charles Haddon Spurgeon began his ministry in London most Baptist and Congregational churches were quiet and subdued and even the Methodists had largely lost their original fire. These groups in general still held to the evangelical faith, but the preaching lacked fervor, the churches possessed little vitality, and most were happy to merely keep the even tenor of their way. Frequent flyer syndrome.

This trap is so subtle that many churches enter and are made captive unawares. No church ever took purposeful action to adopt the frequent flyer syndrome as its operational objective. It just happens. A dull routine sets in. A monotonous predictability becomes almost sacred. A sense of boredom seems normal. The church moves off the edge and onto the ledge.

The frequent flyer syndrome can be cured. It is not universally fatal. It does require treatment. Perhaps the surgical removal of some "sacred cow" programs or the sometimes painful process of making healthy some aspects of church life that are weak and anemic. It may even cost the loss of some folk whose comfort level is so dependent on the familiar and predictable that changes even in the pursuit of Great Commission fulfillment are unacceptable. At a minimum, it demands an honest answer to the "why are we doing what we are doing" question.

Changes will occur in attitude and mind-set first. Not everyone will recognize the need for change or welcome change if the need is recognized. We are all familiar with the 80/20 principle. It tells us that 80 percent of the work is done by 20 percent of the people; 80 percent of the money is given by 20 percent of the people; 80 percent of the trouble is caused by 20 percent of the people (not the same 20 percent!).

There is also the 90/10 principle. It asserts that 90 percent of the people are influenced by the other 10 percent. In other words, a new mind-set for ministry can be developed in your church if about 10 percent of the people buy into the concept. You don't need them all. You don't need half of them. Only 10 percent. A tithe always makes a difference. Do the math for your church. You and a few in the pulpit and pew can become a model for the many.

> *At a minimum, it demands an honest answer to the "why are we doing what we are doing" question.*

Go ahead and begin the resuscitation process. Don't wait for everyone to be on board. It only takes a spark to get a fire going. If you are in a frequent flyer syndrome church, become a quiet catalyst dedicated to a reawakening. Be one of the 10 percent. You can make a difference.

The outward and obvious changes may only be

incremental at first. Too much too soon is exactly that—too much too soon. A frequent flyer syndrome church did not get that way overnight. It will not be redirected overnight.

Thriving churches will pay a price to refocus priorities in such a way that the current congregation will, in time, largely be possessed with a first generation passion. Seeing solid administration, good programing and fine facilities as only means to an end and not an end in themselves, thriving churches will experience relevant and dynamic ministry from the bonding of the foundation of their fathers' faith with a deep commitment to genuine salt and light ministry today.

> *You and a few in the pulpit and pew can become a model for the many.*

Thriving churches will be peopled largely with those whose experience with the Master is fresh and invigorating, whether they are new followers or old-timers. The quality of personal spiritual formation will be such that linked with the sensitivity of a Spirit-filled pastor, an air of "first-time" expectation will prevail.

No call is being issued here for the toxic faith symptom of an emotional high for its own sake. There are those "Christians" who church-hop in perpetual pursuit of some nifty new program or the latest emotional buzz. Such persons make no meaningful contribution to a church and never reach their hard sought after utopia. Their compulsive search for the never-never land of permanent mountaintop living leaves them with a faith that is frothy. These folk are frequent flyers of a different kind. They frequently fly from one church to the next, offering neither stability nor sustained involvement. These people are not the stuff of surviving or thriving churches. They might best be described as a friendly liability.

My lifelong friend John went to pastor a frequent flyer syndrome church about eight years ago. The average attendance was in the 50s. His vision was cast for a thriving church. A few of the fifty bought into the vision. The 90/10 principle at work. New ministries were launched. Some worked and some did not. Those that did were fed and those that did not were starved. People were won to the Lord. The congregation began to grow. A new sanctuary was built. Staff were added. A recent high day saw more than 450 in attendance and the average has now reached nearly 300.

I was there not long ago. The building is quite adequate. The location is good. The population base is strong. The pastoral family is of better than average quality. Excitement was in the air. Expectancy was a way of life. Vibrancy could be felt in the very atmosphere. No frequent flyer syndrome here. All were on a journey that was unpredictable in the most joyous sense of the word. An inspiration. A "first-time" spirit.

The attitude of "first-time" expectation will be a trait of thriving churches. It is within the reach of us all. It is not a matter of gifts or talents, location or population base. It's a matter of the heart. *SEIZE THE DAY!*

CHAPTER TWO

A THRIVING CHURCH WILL . . .

BALANCE THE TUG OF TRADITION WITH THE REALITIES OF RELEVANCE

LIBERAL CHRISTIANS HAVE TOO OFTEN
FORSAKEN REVELATION FOR RELEVANCE AND
CONSERVATIVE CHURCHES HAVE FORSAKEN
RELEVANCE FOR REVELATION.[6]

—LEITH ANDERSON

"... cling to what is good" Romans 12:6.

They cannot join our church unless they do everything just as we have always done. They must accept all our ways. They must conform fully. Such was the attitude of the Pharisees at the Jerusalem Council as recorded in Acts 15. New believers were clashing with the old ways. The specific issue was whether or not the new converts, who were Gentiles, were to be required to undergo physical circumcision.

Paul addressed the tension of his day by pointing out that the heart being transformed was the key issue and that it was not reasonable or necessary to require of new converts what the old fathers themselves were not able to bear. James brought the group to a true New Testament position when he said in Acts 15:19, "It is my judgment, therefore, that we should not make it difficult for the Gentiles who are turning to God".

In thriving churches, new believers will clash with the old ways. In churches that merely survive, the attitude of the Pharisees will prevail ... "They must accept all our ways. They must conform fully." In churches that truly thrive, the spirit of James will dominate. "... we should not make it difficult for the Gentiles turning to God."

For the "we must survive" mentality church, this issue may not be in sharp focus since the majority of whatever growth that occurs will be largely biological or transfer. In the truly thriving church that is experiencing growth through conversion, the old ways and the new believer will provide a constant point of positive tension. Such points of tension, while holding the possibility of disaster, are welcome reminders to those facing such challenges that the church is being built and new birth is occurring.

To successfully respond to these challenges will require both leaders and followers with a commitment to the Great Commission that transcends a commitment to tradition and the "old ways." There is a double-edged danger here. On the one hand some will suggest trashing all traditions in pursuit of relevance and will end up with no point of societal impact and few people. The faithful will be lost and the searcher will find no meaning and will be unable to catch a breath of new life in the vacuum that has been created.

Conversely, there is the companion danger of refusing to adjust or abandon any traditions under the guise of spirituality. Change and compromise are viewed interchangeably and therefore no change is spiritual and God-honoring. A fortress mentality sets in. The numbers dwindle. There is no point of societal impact. The faithful who are unable to cope with any change continue to patch the fortress but no one is attacking from without. The fortress is collapsing from within. The searcher may drop in but will not stay, unable to catch a breath of new life in the suffocating atmosphere.

I have with interest and a genuine sense of respect visited various Amish communities. The somewhat nostalgic scene of the Amish family in their distinctive dress and trademark single horse buggy is familiar to all of us. No cars. No tractors to toil the land. No electricity. No telephones. No churches. Uniform dress requirements. And all in the name of their religious beliefs.

Many from a more "enlightened" perspective say that these things are of no significance. They ought not to be required of people. With benign delight, some observe the Amish way of life and then retreat to their relative affluence with a sense of smugness reflecting an attitude that says such requirements are ridiculous and extreme.

Could a new believer who had three wives keep them all or must he set aside two and keep only his favorite? Was he to select his senior wife and dismiss his junior wives thereby forcing them into prostitution as the only way to eke out an existence? Or could he select one of his younger junior wives and force the older and more senior wives onto the street? What about the children? These were the questions posed to a regional conference in Africa where I had the responsible privilege of serving as chairman. Questions that were vital and timely in the culture. Questions demanding a response. Questions that tended to weaken the knees of the fainthearted. That such matters should even be an item of legitimate discussion at a church conference seems totally foreign to those of us from America. There are those who would hold that to even formalize discussion on the topic is impossible and immoral.

> *The gospel cannot be detached from the culture in which it is presented.*

And then there are the middle-class Christians in America. Possessors of cars and cottages; boats and buildings; stocks and bonds; restaurants and resorts; toys of all sizes for boys of all ages. Could it be that the Amish or the African might with accuracy look at our affluence and our "much goods stored up for many days" and say ridiculous, extreme, impossible and immoral?

The gospel cannot be detached from the culture in which it is presented. The lifestyle application of the gospel cannot reasonably be expected to uniformly and universally reflect the styles and mores of a particular generation, a particular culture or a particular generational style or slice in time. Major church fights have developed and denominations have even been formed over just such issues. Churches that thrive will successfully answer the question of whether the lifestyle positions held by them and expected of new believers are biblically based, culturally curved or simply historically handed down.

> *Churches that thrive will successfully answer the question of whether the lifestyle positions held by them and expected of new believers are biblically based, culturally curved, or simply historically handed down.*

Francis Schaffer in his book *The Great Evangelical Disaster* said,

> Ours is a post-Christian world in which Christianity is no longer the consensus or ethos of our society. The evangelical accommodation to the world of our age represents the removal of the last barrier against the breakdown of our culture.[7]

It is not a question of whether the church needs lifestyle standards. We must be a crosscurrent in our culture. We must be salt and light, but our positions must be biblically based, not merely hollow traditions to be defended.

The curator of a museum explained that the reason for disappearance of the dinosaur was its inability to turn the corner when history did. A thriving church will turn the corner of relevant ministry, being able to discern what must be preserved for the gospel's sake and what can, and perhaps should, be shed from the traditionalism of the past. As George Barna put it,

> It will be increasingly difficult to convince the unchurched, and those who are questioning Christianity, that our faith is pertinent to the 21st century if the tools of our trade are from the last century.[8]

A thriving church will practice tolerance while preserving tradition. It was Charles Swindoll who wrote, "Tradition is the living faith of those now dead; traditionalism is the dead faith of those now living."[9]

One of the devil's masterstrokes is that of dividing forces that ought to stand together. He has enjoyed noticeable success at this strategy. On the tradition vs. relevance question, many churches have splintered and ground themselves to sawdust unable to agree on what was a principle of the Word and what was a transitory whim of the local culture.

This is a call for balance. I am aware of a recent situation where a minister had his credentials revoked because he wore a short-sleeved shirt on his denomination's campground. No balance. Conversely, more than one major religious body in the United States has recently passed legislation or issued official admonitions urging acceptance into full membership and ministry of those practicing a homosexual or lesbian lifestyle. No balance.

In my judgment, both of these positions are

improper. One, because it overinterprets the Bible and arrives at a position that cannot be rationally defended. The other, because it underinterprets the Bible and clearly walks away from scriptural instruction and commands in an attempt to placate a humanistic culture. Both are extreme. Both lack balance.

While most of us are not in danger of either extreme, it is always a struggle to avoid tipping over the emotional edge when our historic positions are challenged or questioned. In this dynamic decade, thriving churches will constantly face these issues as civilized pagans come to Christ. Battles must be waged over major issues only. Internal skirmishes over traditions or guerilla warfare over the nonessential are both tricks of the evil one.

> *Internal skirmishes over traditions or guerilla warfare over the nonessential are both tricks of the evil one.*

If a Saturday evening service would minister to more people than a Sunday evening service, when should the evening service be held? Is it important for a man to wear a suit to church? Is adultery always wrong? Is the King James the "real" Bible? Is homosexual behavior a sin or a sickness? Is it important for a lady to wear a dress or skirt to church? Do we go to movies? Should those who minister in song be believers? Is it okay to eat out on Sunday? Is gossip a sin? Is abortion murder? Can a Christian drink wine? Is a barbecue on Sunday okay? Is it always wrong to lie?

The listing of questions of this kind is seemingly endless. Some of these questions are of eternal significance. Some are not. Sometimes questions like these reflect an honest, searching heart. Sometimes the responses to such questions reflect a concrete mind—all mixed up and permanently set! Some people bring such questions forward only to push as far as possible and not in the attitude of a sincere searcher. Facing these matters will require our best wisdom, gentle understanding and discernment.

A thriving church will approach these matters seeking biblical guidance. A "we must survive" church will not approach them at all or if approached it will be with a pre-established outcome and a deadly predictable response. To some of these issues, the Bible speaks with clarity, and thriving churches must stand with those injunctions regardless of society's headlong drive to legitimize evil in the name of progress and non-discrimination. To others of these questions, the Bible does not speak. Tradition has a strong voice however. The tendency to apply cultural expectations of another generation to the present in the name of godliness and holiness seems more spiritual than the culture-driven model but can be just as destructive.

In some cases the answers will continue to be clear-cut. For others, we may with some discomfort come to surrender long-held preferences in the name of vital ministry to today's hurting people. This is not an easy task or a journey without potholes. It is truly a matter of the heart. We can do this.

In 1803 the British government created a Civil Service position and hired a man to fill it. His responsibility was to station himself over the white cliffs of Dover at the south of England. Specifically, he was to be a lookout for the French navy. An invasion was suspected and even expected under the leadership of the French Emperor, Napoleon. If the lookout saw the French approaching, he was to warn the nearby garrison to prepare to defend their island nation.

At the conclusion of World War II in 1945, it was discovered that the British were still paying a man to watch for the French navy that might be carrying Napoleon's troops. The little Frenchman had been dead about 100 years and obviously posed no military or any other kind of threat but we have always done it like this! Relevance no longer demanded the continuance of a long-held tradition. The times and the needs had changed!

Some things must never change. Some things must soon change. Some beliefs are God's Word to us. Some beliefs are our words to ourselves. God's Word to us is inspired, divine and eternal. Our words to ourselves are rarely any of these things.

Surviving and thriving churches agree entirely that God's Word is an absolute. The tension is injected into our discussion when the focus turns to our word to ourselves. As one well-known adage admonishes, *in essentials, unity; in nonessentials, tolerance; in all things, charity.*

This is a call for balance. Extremes have always existed and cripple the church yet today.

I know of a situation where, years ago, a man came to Christ and was genuinely converted. Two or three of his teeth were gold-filled. Since gold was then viewed as "worldly" his pastor insisted that he have the gold fillings removed and replaced with amalgam fillings. In the name of spirituality, the man agreed and the gold disappeared. No balance. On the other hand, I know a man who lived a long-term life of sin and drunkenness, all the while professing to be a part of the family of the redeemed. Rarely went to church. Wasted his substance with riotous living. Spent many weekends in a drunken stupor while claiming to be a follower of the Master. No balance. Neither of these situations reflected reason. They were extreme. We must not compound errors of this type. Balance.

Balancing the tug of tradition with the realities of relevance is no easy task. Thriving churches will do so, however. It is not a matter of gifts or talents, location or population base. It's a matter of the heart. *SEIZE THE DAY!*

CHAPTER THREE

A Thriving Church Will . . .

CLOSE THE DISTANCE TO THE DESTITUTE

If we aspire to live like Jesus, our lives should have an element of chosen hardship because we desire to grow in character and want to identify with those less fortunate than ourselves.[10]

PAUL BORTHWICK

"... be willing to associate with people of low position"
Romans 12:16.

The preaching of the gospel and various social
expressions of ministry were twins in the early days of
the evangelical movement in North America. Abolition
of slavery, orphanages, inner-city missions, soup
kitchens, and a host of other social needs captured both
the attention and the action of our forebears.

A hymn of Grace Noll Crowell reflects the activist
attitude that preceded our day. She wrote,

Because I have been given much, I too must give.
Because of Thy great bounty, Lord, each day I live,
I shall divide my gifts from Thee
With all the people that I see
Who have the need of help from me.
Because I have been sheltered, fed, by Thy good care,
I cannot see another's lack and I not share
My glowing fire, my loaf of bread,
My roof's safe shelter overhead,
That each, too, may be comforted.

At some nonspecific time in the rather recent past of
the evangelical movement a subtle evolutionary thought
process shift took place. We would concentrate on the
preaching of the Word and winning people to Jesus and
let the "liberal" churches care for the social ministry
needs. In fact, the term "social gospel" came to have a
thoroughly distasteful connotation. To be involved in
social ministry almost left one's reputation suspect in the
born again circle.

Our first priority then is our first priority now—to
preach the gospel. Churches that thrive will continue to

issue a clarion call to salvation from their pulpits and by their people. They will also, however, evidence a heightened awareness of and involvement in compassionate response to the crushing social needs in our society. They will, in the words of Romans, *". . . be willing to associate with people of low position."*

Richard Wilke, United Methodist Bishop of Arkansas, in a book entitled *And Are We Yet Alive?* said,

> We have forgotten the poor, the dispossessed, the ethnic minorities, the people with handicapping conditions right in our own hometowns. We pass resolutions about the poor, but we do not invite them to our churches. We give bread, but we do not break bread with them.[11]

> *Our first priority then is our first priority now—to preach the gospel.*

One of the most fascinating and convicting scriptures for me is found in Matthew 11:4-5. The Master is speaking,

> Go back and report to John what you see: The blind receive sight, the lame walk and those with leprosy are cured, the deaf hear, the dead are raised and the good news is preached to the poor.

This verse is a litany of the miraculous. The blind receive sight—a miracle! The lame walk—a miracle! Those with leprosy are cured—a miracle! The deaf hear—a miracle! The dead are raised—a miracle! The good news is preached to the poor—a miracle?

All of the things listed by Matthew to be reported to John by his followers require direct, overt and easily identified divine intervention except the preaching of the good news to the poor. Ministry to the poor, however they may be described, is within our grasp. Not only in our grasp but also in our pool of responsibility. It may have appeared in the miraculous list of Matthew 11 as a result of the Master peering down the long halls of history and observing the disgusting tendency of the affluent North American late 20th century church to again give the places of prominence to the wealthy and the places of dishonor to the poor. Troublingly similar to the Pharisees.

Many contemporary polls and surveys reveal that Americans will respond positively to volunteering in the coming years. This commendable societal trait will be further reinforced when persons already inclined toward service as a result of cultural tendency are born again. Then the compassion of Christ is added to the tendency to volunteer that already exists and a great force for God and good results. Thriving churches will capitalize on this latent desire to be of service, not just for the good of our fellowman but in the spirit of Christ.

Surviving churches will attempt to re-enlist the tired faithful while thriving churches will augment this tried and tested work force with these who have so recently met the Master face-to-face. While surviving churches will focus their service on themselves by caring for the disadvantaged within their own circle, thriving churches will go beyond and in addition to such necessary and commendable internal service will reach out to their communities in a variety of ways.

They went on follow-up visitation in the poor section of a large Southern city. The children from the family had been to vacation Bible school but the parents had never attended the church. During the visit, it became apparent that the children had no footwear. One of the visitors from the church inquired and found that the kids, in fact, had no shoes.

She took a piece of paper and asked each child in turn to stand on it so that she could trace the outline of their feet. Having completed that task she excused herself, promising to return soon. She took the paper to a nearby shoe store and informed the clerk that she wanted good quality sneakers to fit those feet. She returned to the home and gave the children each a personal pair of new sneakers and left.

When recounting the story after returning to the church she was asked how the mother responded. She said that the mother with tears streaming down her face asked, "May I come to your church?"

Robert Fulghum in his book *It Was On Fire When I Lay Down On It*, poses this troubling observation:

> Do you know that we spend a couple of million dollars a year on dog food alone in this country? About twice as much as we do for baby food for people. Dog food accounts for about 11 percent of supermarket sales of dry groceries. The average supermarket chain devotes more than one hundred feet of shelf space to dog food and doggy needs. Doggy burgers and doggy bits and chicken a la dog and puppy yum yums and all the rest of it. Take a look sometime. Seven and a half billion pounds total of pet food a year. Ninety percent of the dogs in this country eat and live better than 75 percent of the people in this world.[12]

This is not an anti-dog paragraph. This is a testimony to lack of balance. More for dogs than for needy humanity is impossible to defend—rationalize maybe—but not defend. Our hearts must be touched not only by cute pets but also by crushed people.

Thriving churches will view their facilities as a command post from which the church goes out to minister. Surviving churches will view their facilities as the church and those who want ministry had better show up.

Thriving churches will view their facilities as a combination of brick and mortar assembled into a building from which and in which ministry occurs. Ministry will take precedence over buildings. Surviving churches will tend to view their facilities as a museum. A place to visit and observe but not to be touched. The maintenance of the building and grounds, which is in fact a valuable ministry, will tend to be seen in surviving churches as "the" ministry.

> *Our hearts must be touched not only by cute pets but also by crushed people.*

"No Children in the Sanctuary" signs are never found in thriving churches. The this-is-my-seat-sit-somewhere-else attitude is never found in thriving churches. Surviving churches may not only fail to minister to the destitute, they may become destitute themselves but of a different poverty. A poverty of the spirit is much to be dreaded.

Clothing for the destitute, lodging for the homeless, staffing the kitchen at the inner-city mission, shelter for battered spouses and children, groceries for the hungry, gas for the car of the stranded, alcohol and drug rehabilitation centers, AIDS victims support groups, prison fellowship, the many and varied pro-life issues—these are only a few of the many avenues of ministry open to all churches. The possibilities for involvement in the name of the Master seem endless.

There is neither need nor rationale for a church believing it must begin a new ministry to all these and other divergent groups. To attempt to begin and support new ministries to the endless groups that need genuine ministry would tax into oblivion the assets of most churches. In many areas, viable ministry is occurring to the destitute through existing structures and organizational networks. Thriving churches will often support and cooperate with these existing structures since the objective is ministry in the name of the Master not merely in the name of the church.

Again, this is a call for balance. The evangelical movement has in recent history been noticeably under-involved in ministry to the needs of society. The danger always exists of overcorrection. There is a well known tendency of people and churches to overswing the pendulum when change is identified as necessary and undertaken. Such extremes must be avoided.

To clearly preach the gospel message and lead people to Christ but at the same time show no interest in and have no involvement in active ministry aimed at society's great needs reflects a lack of balance. To see the meeting of society's great needs as the fulfillment of the gospel is a point of view equally out of balance. In these dynamic days, thriving churches will wed the two in a balanced and harmonious union. The gospel must always be first but never alone. Society's needs must never be first but always included. Balance.

There is another side of this issue against which the thriving church must be on guard. There are those who are so committed to the attempt to meet the needs of society that they would put others on a guilt trip who do not see such ministry as their one and only passion. Such well-intentioned dragons will often dispense an emotional appeal that is shortsighted and narrow. To follow the driving wedge of their thinking to its logical outcome would lead to the conclusion that the only truly valuable ministry is to the destitute. After all, is it not easier for a camel to pass through the eye of a needle than for a rich man to go to heaven?

> *The gospel must always be first but never alone. Society's needs must never be first but always included. Balance.*

Such an approach is also out of balance. To pursue only the affluent lacks biblical support. To pursue only the destitute lacks biblical support. To be aware of the needs around us and do all within our reasonable ability to minister appropriately to those in need regardless of their standing in society is clearly a biblical principle.

Then there are those on the other end of the continuum. Gun-shy of most attempts at any ministry to the destitute. After all it's often difficult or virtually impossible to verify bona fide need and besides such ministry offers no hope to build our local church. Then there are the professional con-artists who always hit on the churches for a handout.

While pastoring some years ago I was contacted by a woman who said that she and her family were in great need of groceries. The situation, she said, was a crisis. I made an appointment to go and see her at her apartment. There was only one or two cans of food in the cupboard. I was startled by the empty shelves. Our church provided some groceries that day.

Later that week I attended a city ministerial meeting. Some of the men there were discussing a certain woman who called more than a few of them looking for groceries. Her name and address were terribly familiar to me. Her scam, as it turned out, was to store groceries under the bed and leave only a few in the cupboard. She would then call a minister, request a handout and suggest that the minister come to her apartment to verify that she truly was in need. I took marginal consolation in the fact that I was one of several that were stung by her scam. Misery really does love company.

Was our church now to adopt a no-groceries-for-anyone-we-don't-know policy. No! We had been taken, no doubt. But real need still existed in our community. Safety checks were put in place. Ministry to those in need did not stop because of one rather slick con-artist.

I was driving through a southern city recently and out of the corner of my eye caught a moving sight. An old car sat by the side of the road. A woman and two small children milled aimlessly around the car. The husband and father was out near the road displaying a homemade sign. "No money. Will work for Food. Any Job." I did not live in that city. I could offer no work. It was impossible to judge if he was on the level. I drove past him and did not stop. "Inasmuch as you have done it unto one of the least of these . . . you have done it unto me." It popped into my head. Was that God speaking or am I just a soft touch? It troubled me. I turned around and went back . . . gave him $10 . . . not much . . . one meal at McDonald's maybe. He was very appreciative. He felt good—I felt better.

Thriving churches will close the distance to the destitute. It's not a matter of gifts or talents, location or population base. It's a matter of the heart. *SEIZE THE DAY!*

CHAPTER FOUR

A Thriving Church Will . . .

DISCIPLE AND DEPLOY ITS PEOPLE LIKE AN ARMY, NOT MERELY COLLECT THEM IN THE SUNDAY FORTRESS

The true measure of any society is not what it knows but what it does with what it knows.[13]

—Warren Bennis

We refuse to become the "rabbit hole" Christians John Stott speaks of, popping out of our holes and racing from our insulated caves to all-Christian gatherings only to run back again.[14]

—Charles Swindoll

"... serving the Lord" Romans 12:11.

Frederick Wentz in some of his writings said,

The church needs to view itself as paratroopers dropped behind enemy lines on Monday with the expectation of making their way back to the supply depot the following Sunday.[15]

There is no doubt that thriving churches will both believe and behave in ministry beyond their walls. The real issue being addressed here is not the need to be involved in overt ministry beyond the walls. As discussed in an earlier chapter, such ministry is both valid and necessary. It will be one of the trademarks of thriving churches. The questions to address are how to prepare for "outside the walls" ministry and what form such ministry will assume. It is a given that "outside the walls" ministry will occur and be a part of the life cycle of thriving churches. C. S. Lewis once said,

Enemy occupied territory—that's what the world is. Christianity is the story of how the rightful King has landed in disguise and is calling us all to take part in a great campaign of sabotage.

Those who understand the gifts of the Spirit tell us that they believe only about ten percent of believers possess the gift of evangelism. If this premise is accepted, only one in ten is truly gifted in the one-on-one deliberate encounter of sharing the faith. For the vast majority of Christians then, our most effective witness may not be in the context of organized soul-winning visitation. Whether at the workplace or in some less structured social setting, we must surely recognize that we all have a responsibility to walk through open witnessing doors that the Master, in His providence, places before us. Perhaps a fellow employee, a family member, a neighbor or the passenger seated beside us on the airplane. In His timing, God often allows our lives to briefly intersect the life path of another in need. In such settings, we must be both sensitive and courageous.

This is not intended to reflect in any way on organized "cold turkey" visitation programs. Such ministry will continue to occur in some circles but not at the high-pitched level of the past. While involvement in such programs is sometimes negatively motivated and guilt driven, there is no doubt that people have been won to the Lord as a result of such activity. But the ratio between effort exerted and results realized is not very inspiring. I once heard a speaker reporting on a cold turkey visitation program that revealed one person converted, discipled and incorporated into the church for every eight hundred and three visits.

> *In His timing, God often allows our lives to briefly intersect the life path of another in need.*

However, it seems that for many, an authentic Christian life fleshed out in the marketplace under the pressure of working with nonbelievers is where the impact for the Master can best be demonstrated. True followers of Christ will stand in contrast with much of the value system displayed in his workday environment. It is so vital that we do not appear to be defending the unnecessary or to be only Sunday believers, no different from the others where money and morals are concerned.

There is a societal suspicion directed towards

Christians in America, largely as a result of the moral collapse of high profile Christian personalities. The infamy of the moral collapse has been exacerbated by the pious and disgusting rationalization of clearly non-Christian behavior by those claiming to be in the service of the King of Kings. It is no wonder that the world looks somewhat askance at our claim that God's ways are best ways.

> *Your talk walks and your walk talks but your walk talks louder than your talk walks.*

The general distrust towards the church is complicated by believers in name whose day-to-day conduct in the business place lacks the marks of integrity and high ethics. There are those who hold the position that the "average Christian" cannot be differentiated from the "average sinner" in the workplace in terms of work ethic and basic honesty. Ted Engstrom once said, "Some of the best fiction of our day can be found on the expense reports of Christian businessmen."[16] It could and should be hotly debated as to how true such allegations may or may not be. The fact that such issues are perceived as truth makes them so in the eyes of many.

Such perceptions are not corrected and overcome by good intentions or by announcements from the pulpit or pronouncements from some faraway denominational office. They are overcome by true believers from thriving churches fleshing out their faith with integrity in the caldron of day-to-day late 20th century living. It's the walk and talk issue. Your talk walks and your walk talks but your walk talks louder than your talk walks.

A thriving church will deploy its people into the world every day with a mission to live an authentic Christian life in an ever increasing hedonistic and materialistic society. The people around us must clearly be able to identify a difference in the followers of Christ from nonbelievers in our influence, our integrity and our industry. Such genuine Christian conduct in the workplace attracts people to the Master.

His name is Leo. He attended the first church I pastored. A man of quiet disposition and sensitive spirit who was the same steady Christian at the factory through the week as he was in the church on Sunday. Once when I was visiting with an unsaved young man in the sphere of influence of our church, he volunteered the observation that if he ever became a Christian he wanted to be one like Leo. He worked with Leo at the factory. He saw him in the "real" world of the workplace and what he saw convinced him that this Christianity stuff really did make a difference in people's lives. Thriving churches will deploy such "real" ambassadors of the faith day after day after day and as a result of their influence the faith will spread and the family will expand.

In the significant work *The Day America Told The Truth* the surveys conducted by the authors revealed many things about us as a people. Only 13 percent of us believe in all of the Ten Commandments. Forty percent of us believe in five of the Ten Commandments. There is no moral consensus in the country at this time. Thirty-two percent of the respondents believe that they have been lied to by a minister and 91 percent of the respondents said that they lie regularly.

This is the values-deprived culture into which our soldiers and ambassadors go every day to live out a

Christian lifestyle. Thriving churches will equip their people to face this moral vacuum in our society which is not unlike a society long ago about which it was said, "everyone did as he saw fit" (Judges 21:25).

> *Thriving churches will adequately train their people to be effective witnesses for Christ in the marketplace.*

Effective discipleship will be the watershed proving ground for surviving vs. thriving churches at this point. Believers lacking appropriate grounding and discipleship cannot be successfully and regularly launched into the semi-hostile environment of the workplace. Without training, the believer may tend to withdraw out of lack of confidence and fall into the I'm-a-Christian-but-they-can't-tell-it mind-set. Or the believer may tend to exude an artificial and plastic brand of Christianity that is seen by the sinner for what it is—artificial and plastic. Or the believer may come across as the narrow, morally superior, overly pious type and therefore disgusting.

Thriving churches will adequately train their people to be effective witnesses for Christ in the marketplace. Surviving churches will quickly agree that such training is necessary and to be desired but will never quite get around to offering the training. Dying churches will believe such training to be unnecessary and will recommend just "trusting God" to bring in the non-believer.

Once again this is a call for balance. Balance between discipleship and deployment. One without the other is inadequate and really counterproductive. Lack of balance leads toward an out of focus perspective on reality. Heavy discipleship without deployment is no more to be pursued than aggressive deployment lacking discipleship.

Discipleship without deployment results in an artificial spirituality and mock maturity that very often leads ultimately to internal friction in the church. The fruits of discipleship are internalized within the fellowship and the irresistible urge to measure and inspect each other slowly takes hold. Lacking a clear focus on deployment, the ever fattening disciples adopt little tests to prove their discipleship. How many books did you read this week? How many mornings were you at the 6:00 a.m. prayer meeting? How many small groups are you attending? How many groups are you leading?

Discipleship is like a lake. Lacking an outlet, it stagnates. With only inflow and no outflow, the lake comes to exist for its own sake and loses genuine purpose in the broader scheme of things. There is such a place in the Middle East well known to us all—the Dead Sea. All in and no out. You can float but you can't drink.

True discipleship equips people to share the living water with others so that they too may drink. True discipleship does not merely fatten the participants so that they may float on the dead sea of their own spiritual pride. Hymn poets and chorus writers have more than once caught the outflow theme. They would have us sing that God's love is like a river of life flowing out from me, or of being channels only.

The Lake of Discipleship is a vital link in the life chain of spreading the good news. In spite of the fact that the lake may be beautiful in its own right, it is understood from the beginning that its true purpose is to flow out. No reason to exist for its own sake. The lake is the birthplace of the broad river that flows below. The Lake of Discipleship is the birth place of the River of Deployment that leads to the broadening and expansion of the family of faith on down the line.

> *Heavy discipleship without deployment is no more to be pursued than aggressive deployment lacking discipleship.*

For a number of years my family and I had the privilege of living just a few miles from the "Father of Waters." This mighty river flows some 2,330 miles from northern Minnesota to the Gulf of Mexico, invading that body of water about 80 miles southeast of New Orleans. It serves as the master drainage stream for the area lying between the Rocky Mountains and the Appalachian region and has a drainage basin of some 1.2 million square miles. It is the third longest river system in the world after the Nile and the Amazon. The Mississippi. Impressive to visit, especially downstream. Wide and expansive. We all know of the mighty Mississippi.

But what about Lake Itasca? It is located in Clearwater County in northwestern Minnesota and is at an elevation of 1,670 feet above sea level. Lake Itasca is the mother of the "Father of Waters." It is here that the mighty Mississippi begins its long and strong journey to the Gulf and then on to the shores of the world. Lake Itasca gives birth to the Mississippi River. Not just once at some distant point in history. Every day. In the perpetual process of giving birth to the larger unit, Lake Itasca is virtually unknown except to trivial pursuit types and true Gophers. The Mississippi receives the waters of more than 100 tributaries on its winding way to the Gulf. The return for Lake Itasca is more than 100 to 1.

Such is the ideal relationship between discipleship and deployment. The Lake of Discipleship gives birth to the River of Deployment, not just once in a 13-week blitz campaign but every day. Many tributaries are swept into the building current as it moves along with growing strength and gains both width and depth. Discipleship may be eclipsed by the results of the forces deployed as they are increasingly effective in seeing new converts enter the family. The focus of celebration is on the new believers and the growing church that results. Without Lake Itasca we would not have the mighty Mississippi River. Without true discipleship, effective deployment with lasting results is not possible.

> *As discipleship must have an outlet, so deployment must have a feeder.*

The lake and the river are a balanced and mutually dependent team. The lake without an outlet will in time die. The river without a feeder will in time dry up. Neither outcome is desirable. Both outcomes plague surviving churches and sound the death knell for dying churches. As discipleship must have an outlet, so deployment must have a feeder.

Deployment efforts lacking trained "deployees" may enjoy initial success as they run on start-up momentum or on the leader's charisma. Lacking sound discipleship, however, such efforts will in time crash and burn. There are many pitfalls in premature or pressured deployment. These include but are certainly not limited to:

1. Sending babes to battle—expecting too much from a new convert too soon. This pitfall capitalizes on the amazing energy of the new convert. Since many old-timers have lost some of their early zeal, there is a strong urge to draft these troops early and send them to battle armed only with a new faith and a fresh heart. The time that would be required to train and disciple seems a waste. High mortality rate results. A short burst of progress is later eclipsed by picking up the burned-out pieces of a crashed crusader.

2. Sending old-timers to battle—assuming that the faithful have the goods. Merely being around the church for a long time does not indicate that discipleship has occurred. While a certain amount of maturity happens as a result of the roll of the calendar, deliberate effort must occur to move the faithful to maturity. I would not want to be operated on by a heart surgeon who had merely spent a lot of time at medical school. I would much prefer one who had taken the course, absorbed the material and graduated. The time to train and disciple is assumed to be unnecessary. As one wag suggested, we should never assume anything except a four percent mortgage. Thriving churches will not afford themselves the luxury of assuming that longevity and maturity are synonymous. High frustration results. Why wasn't I taught? How could they have been here so long and know so little?

3.   Sending no one to battle—waiting until everyone is perfectly and fully trained. The fear of failure often drives a desire for perfectionism that freezes into inactivity the very thing it was supposed to mobilize. If we wait to deploy our people purposefully into the workplace until all signals are strong green, we will never get it done. When we are somewhat discouraged with efforts to train and disciple with an eye to deployment, we must take both heart and action. Almost every good idea seems like a bad idea about halfway through the implementation process. There comes a time when we must take the plunge. Thriving churches will disciple and deploy. Not one or the other. Both. Balance.

Thriving churches will not agree on the discipleship material or methods that should be utilized. Thriving churches will not agree on the deployment methods and mechanics that should be utilized. On these two things, however, they will unanimously agree. Thriving churches will be committed to and will implement both discipleship and deployment. Methods, material and mechanics are secondary. The mission is primary to the thrivers. The mission can be accomplished only with the yoked team of discipleship and deployment.

Historians tell us that in the time of Christopher Columbus the maps of the world reflected the common theory of the day that the world was flat. Reaching to the end of their knowledge base, cartographers placed notations on the maps at the edge of the known world limits which said, "Beyond here be dragons!" Surviving churches will gather together in an insulated environment and rejoice in each other's company and their common bond through the blood of Christ. They will often reflect a mild panic concerning society and survival and sometimes even be preoccupied with a "Beyond here be dragons!" fatalism.

Thriving churches will gather together in an insulated environment and rejoice in each other's company and their common bond through the blood of Christ. With mild apprehension married to firm resolve they will send out determined disciples who will seek to make a genuine difference for God and good in an environment complete with dragons. Columbus proved the dragon worshipers wrong. Thriving churches will do so as well.

Thriving churches will deploy their people like an army, not merely collect them in the Sunday fortress. The key question is not how many came to church to worship but rather how many left to serve. It's not a matter of gifts or talents, location or population base. It's a matter of the heart. *SEIZE THE DAY!*

CHAPTER FIVE

A Thriving Church Will . . .

ENGAGE IN BATTLE SELECTIVELY

Most church fights aren't over theology or even ministry goals; they're over priorities and methodology.[17]

—Larry Osborne

You can't expect to win people to Christ when the body is fragmented and at war.

—Copied

"If it is possible, as far as it depends on you, live at peace with everyone" Romans 12:18.

". . . listen to my appeal, be of one mind, live in peace" 2 Corinthians 13:11.

While waiting to be seated in a fine restaurant one evening, I was browsing through several books displayed on shelves in the restaurant lobby. One caught my eye in particular. It was entitled *Master Christian* and was authored by Marie Corelli. On the first page were found these words, "Dedicated to all those churches who quarrel in the name of Christ."

Both Paul and Corelli recognized the propensity of churches to fuss. I was once approached by a very influential gentleman who resided in a small town where I was pastoring. There was a total of four churches in our town and this man offered the observation that in his many years in the community he had taken note that every one of those churches at some time or another had become embroiled in internal conflict. Not over some issue that threatened the life and existence of the church as a result of some overt external threat. Rather, over some relatively minor issue of personal preference, style, method, turf protection or power struggle war was waged. And the community knew it. He never attended any of those churches on a regular basis, but in a small town a church fuss was common knowledge.

Surviving churches will engage in battle. Thriving churches will engage in battle. The vital difference will be with whom battle will occur and over what issues. Enemy identification will be a point of disagreement between the survivors and the thrivers. Surviving churches will possess a narrow understanding of the enemy issue and tend to see any person who opposes their way as an enemy. Thriving churches will possess a broad understanding of the enemy issue and will see any person who opposes His way as an agent of the enemy.

> *Surviving churches will engage in battle. Thriving churches will engage in battle. The vital difference will be with whom battle will occur and over what issues.*

Surviving churches will do battle over nonessentials. Regularly. In some cases, with gusto. I have actually observed or been asked to offer a possible road to peace in the following situations, namely:

1. There was the church that experienced noticeable internal tension over what color the ladies' restroom would be painted in the new church then under construction.

2. There were the skirmishes over whether or not to add a fellowship hall that would result in a kitchen being a part of the church facility.

3. Another situation of which I have knowledge experienced no little stress over relocating a shrinking but rigid Sunday school class. They had exercised long-term squatters' rights on prime space in the church, but the growing young adults' class needed larger facilities. Friction.

4. The King James wars come to mind. There is an

acknowledged majesty about the King James Version of the Bible, especially in the poetic books, but the suggestion that Elizabethan English is somehow more sacred than English from other generations was and is a premise lacking rational foundation. The original languages of the Scriptures, after all, did not include English in any form.

5. And then there are sound tracks. Canned music no less. Some thought it was great. Others thought it was grotesque. Pick up sides. Have a fuss.

6. Let's move the evening service time from 7:00 to 6:00 p.m. More young families could come and bring their kids. So went the proposition. No way. If you move the service to 6:00, my family won't be there. It is just not the right time. So went the protest. No flexibility. No give. Nonproductive tension in the air.

7. Are midweek prayer services sacred or silly? The people were committed to them. The pastor was not. They came to pray. He went to play basketball with the youth. Not everyone was happy!

8. I had worn it for more than 20 years. He wanted me to take it off before I spoke in his church. He thought I was trailing the world. I thought he was twisting the wonderful. It was a bit tense. We finally agreed to disagree.

9.   We really should discontinue afternoon services at camp meeting, he suggested. Few people come and the number each year seems on the decline and furthermore it is really not fair to the evangelist. He's right. Hasn't happened yet though. Too much opposition. Too touchy an issue.

10. They still thought that the traditional spring and fall special revival services in the church were the outreach ministry of the fellowship. He knew that was no longer true. Need to fine-tune the focus and thrust of such meetings. Tough to do. Old expectations die hard. Heels get dug in.

> *Surviving churches will do battle over non-essentials. Regularly.*

The illustration list could go on and on ad nauseam. Churches that merely survive will continue to do battle over issues lacking any of the stuff of eternity in them. The battlefield is rarely, almost never, theological. It never seems to involve heretics or any call for a relaxation of accepted biblical principles and cardinal teachings. It is not battle over principle but preference. Not over the Master's teaching but over the method taken. Not over the message of illumination but over the means of implementation.

In the book *All I Really Need To Know I Learned in Kindergarten* the author said that he learned much about life in the kindergarten sandpile. A large portion of what he says he learned there comes to bear on the war and peace issues in the church. He reminds us that some of his childhood lessons included

> Share everything. Play fair. Put things back where
> you found them. Clean up your own mess. Don't
> take things that aren't yours. Say you're sorry when
> you hurt somebody. When you go out into the
> world, watch out for traffic, hold hands and stick
> together. Be aware of wonder. Goldfish and white
> mice and hamsters all die—so do we.[18]

It seems to me that much of the internal friction that often marks a church could be eliminated or removed altogether by checking out the kindergarten sandpile philosophies of life and relationships.

This is, as you might have anticipated by this time in this book, a call for balance. This is not an appeal for a utopian situation in a church where the atmosphere is forever friction-free. Such churches probably don't exist. Disagreement will always exist when two or more humans are in the same place at the same time for an extended period of time. This is not a call for a guilt trip if you are now or have been in a lack of agreement mode with some other person down at the church. Such things are inevitable. Those who share in the ministry of a thriving church will, however, refuse to allow internal disagreements over minor issues to deteriorate into outright warfare. The focus on active, community-impacting ministry will force turf fights, by and large, out of the limelight.

There are those good people who believe or have been taught that disagreements just should not be in the church. The teachings of the New Testament and church history across the ages and until the present moment combine to disprove that notion. Christians just don't always see things eye-to-eye. But neither do

Christians seek to put out the eyes of the other believer with whom they fail to see eye-to-eye. Balance.

A forever friction-free environment is neither normal or necessary. A state of sustained internal warfare whose objective is the destruction of each other is also neither normal or necessary and is sinful. Seek balance.

Those who truly practice balance in this matter of warfare will choose their battles carefully. They will resist being lured into major battle over minor matters. When examples like the ones mentioned earlier in this chapter are held up against the backdrop of the swirling culture around us they make fighting over such issues seem silly at best and sinful at worst.

* Abortion has killed more babies in the USA since 1973 than the total population of Canada.

* One in every 14 Americans say that they would murder for money.

* The AIDS epidemic will touch in some way most American families during the decade, and many church families will be affected.

* Child pornography is a multimillion dollar business in America.

* Spouses are regularly abusing and sometimes killing each other.

* Many children are routinely subject to cruel and devastating sexual, physical and mental abuse.

* Drug abuse is addictive to many, killer to some, makes millions for a few and is invading the safe suburban areas of North America.

* Special interest groups and leaders of some church denominations, under the guise of nondiscrimination and lack of prejudice, are seeking to legitimize the gay

and lesbian lifestyle and "ministry."

Thriving churches will engage in battle with the forces of evil over these issues and others. The influence, action and money of these churches will be brought to bear on items of eternal significance. Through education of their people and participation in groups properly organized to resist these evil forces, thriving churches will wage war where it matters.

This is not the time to engage in battle internally over the color of carpets, classrooms or candles; over class locations or committee selections; over hours of services and the length of sermons. If such issues need to be addressed, then let it be in a proper forum for such discussion and not on the battlefield. It is simply inappropriate to draw life-and-death battle lines over these transitory and temporary matters.

This is not to suggest that differences of opinion will not or should not exist in thriving churches. In reality, such churches will have many and repeated points of tension as the fellowship grows and frequent adjustment occurs. Thriving churches will see such friction for what it is—a positive step in the process of impact ministry to the community. Such tension points must not be allowed to dominate discussion or to cripple or cancel vital ministries.

If the changes suggested call for a shift away from clear biblical teaching or call for a denial of eternal principles, they are to be resisted with all our might. If the changes suggested are merely in methods and functional priorities, keep the cannons covered. People in surviving churches rather routinely wound each other with "friendly fire" in wars over nothing. No winners. Just casualties.

While I was serving as a district superintendent, a decision was made to computerize our district office. Quotes were requested. Demonstrations were endured. A purchase was finally made.

During the demonstration of equipment stage, a lady came to my office to explain why the computer equipment she was selling was clearly superior to the other similar equipment available. Following her presentation, she asked me to explain to her the basic beliefs of The Wesleyan Church.

> *People in surviving churches rather routinely wound each other with "friendly fire" in wars over nothing. No winners. Just casualties.*

Having done my best to appropriately answer her inquiry, she then pressed the point a bit further. How were we different from the Southern Baptists; the Nazarenes; the Christian and Missionary Alliance and several other groups, she wanted to know. Again I did my best to answer. Then she asked the clincher question. "Reverend," she said, "are those churches we just discussed your competition?"

After reflecting for a moment I truly believe the Lord directed me in my answer. "Those churches are not my competition," I replied. "The devil is the competition."

Thriving churches will engage in battle selectively, understanding clearly the identity of the competition. The enemy is not somebody who wants a different color of paint on the restroom wall, the enemy is the devil! It is almost never a question of good versus bad. Rarely are the issues moral or ethical that stand in sharp black-

and-white contrast.

Warren Wiersbe once said, "The devil's masterstroke is that of dividing forces that ought to stand together."[19] There are many that the devil can never defeat. They have decided to follow Jesus. Where the prospects of defeat do not seem to exist, he often attempts to divert and divide. A church diverted from its primary mission or divided over how to implement its mission is just as ineffective in fulfilling the Great Commission as a church that is just plain defeated. The results are the same. None.

Historians tell us that the defeat of egotistical General Custer at the Battle of the Little Big Horn came about in large measure because of dividing forces that should have stood together. Custer divided his command and the Sioux, exercising excellent strategy, attacked the divided force. The outcome is well known. Whether Custer's force as a combined unit could have won the day over Sitting Bull will never be known. This much we do know. Divided, Custer was defeated. The principle still holds.

Thriving churches will understand this principle and will do battle with the devil and his forces, not with each other. It is not a matter of gifts or talents, location or population base. It's a matter of the heart. *SEIZE THE DAY!*

CHAPTER SIX

A Thriving Church Will . . .

FOCUS BOTH PUBLIC AND PRIVATE PRAYER ON ISSUES OF ETERNITY

If we aren't stunned and paralyzed by the need, our prayers can't consume us.[20]

—Mario Murillo

A young boy, ready for bed, interrupted a family gathering in the living room. "I'm going up to say my prayers now. Anybody want anything?"[21]

—Copied

"Be . . . faithful in prayer" Romans 12:12.

* Salvation or surgery

* Conversion or chemotherapy

* Holiness or heart attack

* Fire in the preacher or finances in the plate

* Calling of ministers and missionaries or
  catastrophe of miscarriage or mononucleosis

* Surprising presence of the King or supervising
  person for the kids

If prayer requests were being taken in your church or prayer group, which side of the above list would likely dominate the spoken requests? In surviving churches, the prayer focus is almost entirely on temporal issues, particularly physical health problems. The here and now. In thriving churches the valid concern over physical health and other temporal issues will be balanced with a deep and sincere concern for the salvation of those in the church shadow and those who are a part of its extended family who do not know Christ as personal Savior. The here and now plus the then and there.

I recently did a brief study of the hymns in a certain hymnal listed in the section on prayer. There are 14 selections in the section containing a total of 44 stanzas. Of those 44, only one makes any reference to the matter of prayers for the lost. This hymn by Albert S. Reitz says in the second verse,

Power in prayer, Lord, power in prayer,
Here mid earth's sin and sorrow and care;
Souls lost and dying, souls in despair;
O give me power, power in prayer.

Some time ago I was present in an evening service where the pastor asked for prayer requests. There were 18 spoken requests given and 16 of them were for a wide range of physical matters. Only one was a clear-cut call for prayer for the salvation of an unsaved family member. The request was a tag on a request for a physical need which ended with a by the way, they aren't saved either kind of comment. If one was keeping score it would have read: Here and Now—16, Then and There—1. There was in that group and many others that I have observed little or no sense of urgency over the lost condition of loved ones, neighbors and friends. There is no doubt in my mind that this pastor and people are indeed genuinely concerned over those who do not know the Lord. Concerned but not burdened.

And this church is not unique or unusual when it comes to expressed prayer needs. While I have not counted requests very often, the same disproportionate slant towards the here and now marks the public prayer expression of many a church. This is not a phenomenon of the old or the young; the small town or the big city; this seems to be a broad-based prayer approach that skews and renders fuzzy the potential impact of the church on its knees.

Often the pursuit of the vital is eclipsed by intense activity focused on the good—secondary but good. Such has happened to the prayer focus of many, many churches to the extent that prayers offered for the unsaved are rarely ever heard. The vital is lost as we pursue only the good. Prayers for the safety of our families as they travel. Good. Prayers for those from the church soon to undergo the trauma of a surgical procedure. Good. Prayers for the persons in our fellowship who are battling the horrors of cancer. Good. Prayers for the coworker at the office who had a heart attack. Good. Prayers for those connected with the church who are in military service. Good. Prayers for government leaders. Good. All good but none vital. All good but none eternal.

Could it be that the evangelical movement has been duped by the enemy at this important point? Could it be that the devil might almost welcome prayers for the temporal and physical if such prayers kept the church from focused prayer for the salvation of the lost? Our prayers for all the temporal and health-related issues pose far less threat or challenge to Satan's ultimate objective than do focused and concerted prayers for the salvation of the lost. To our enemy, prayers for the temporal matters are a nuisance while our prayers for salvation of the lost are a direct assault on his purposes.

> *Could it be that the devil might almost welcome prayers for the temporal and physical if such prayers kept the church from focused prayer for the salvation of the lost?*

Then there is the personal, spiritual formation matter. Our own quest for depth and maturity may sometimes become so consuming, that prayers turn almost totally inward. A little chorus from my childhood comes to mind. *My desire, to be like Jesus, my desire, to be like Him. His Spirit fill me, His love*

o'erwhelm me. In deed and word to be like Him.
Absolutely appropriate thought. No subtle suggestion is
offered or implied here that such a pursuit should not
occur. Scrawny Christians will evidence a personal
spiritual formation that is so limited as to render them
emaciated representatives of the Master. No impact on
either the here and now or the then and there.

The inward focused individual is dealing with then
and there issues. How to be personally prepared for
eternity is a major focus of these dear believers. The
problem can arise when the admirable trait of maturity
in Christ is out of balance and the pursuit of personal
holiness eclipses a passion for the lost. Both are matters
of eternity. The feeding of one concern cannot be
allowed to starve the other.

> *It is the intercessory prayers of the saints for
> the salvation of the lost that the enemy
> dreads.*

There are many Christians whose faith is so alive
and whose desire to be Christlike is so sincere, that
living a prayerless life is unthinkable. For such
conscientious believers, one of Satan's most effective
tools may be to divert the prayer effort to the noneternal.
A prayer life so driven by the crisis crush of
circumstance that it centers nearly all prayer effort in
that direction is out of balance. There are certainly
occasions when we are in the vice grip of some
desperate situation that appropriately demands our entire
prayer thrust. But on an ongoing and regular basis, if
our primary prayer focus is only on the temporary and
the physical, the devil has lost little ground. A few

battles perhaps. It is the intercessory prayers of the saints for the salvation of the lost that the enemy dreads. This is not just a battle, this is the war.

Prayer for many of the short-term needs mentioned at prayer request time requires little real effort. A brief request followed by a sincere prayer. Often, that's it. No continued prayer in private for the needs mentioned. We prayed at church and that kind of covers it. It was good that we did pray at church but the word travail as an adjective for prayer could never be faintly considered to apply in these situations. On the other hand, intercessory prayer for the lost is hard work. There is an old Tamil proverb that says, "We must learn to plough deep rather than wide." Heartfelt prayer for the salvation of the lost will narrow our prayer focus and move us deeper rather than wider in prayer scope. A wide and languid river lacks depth and as a result also lacks a powerful current. Narrow the channel, and the river gains depth and the current becomes a force to be reckoned with that sweeps along with it much that would have successfully resisted the weakened and lackadaisical flow of the river when it was wide and shallow.

Intercessory prayer for the salvation of the lost narrows the wide and shallow prayers for every conceivable physical and temporal need into an ever-deepening channel. Power increases as the depth increases. As the channel deepens the increasingly powerful prayer current sweeps along with it many other items that would never have been moved by the wide and shallow prayers focused only on the here and now.

Please do not misunderstand the thrust of this item. Prayer for physical and other temporal needs is both biblically based and one of the benefits of grace in our lives. Many blessings have no doubt been lost and many battles forfeited that could have been won if Christians had more consistently held up to the throne of grace here and now matters. Often when divine intervention follows such prayers, eternal issues are also settled in the afterglow of the Master's moving. God has often performed the clearly miraculous in response to prayers of faith for physical healing. The instances of divine intervention in restoration of marriages, financial miracles and a great variety of other matters is a cause for praise and thanksgiving.

> *Thriving churches will yoke the two oxen of prayer, the here and now and the then and there, into a team pulling a spiritual load together.*

However, in so many churches and prayer fellowships, the overwhelming weight of the prayers is for temporal matters, with eternal issues almost totally neglected or at best, a last minute add-on thought. Too often the prayer focus seems self-directed and perhaps even selfish. It was reported that one man's prayer went thus, "Dear Lord, bless me and my wife, my son John and his wife, we four and no more." It is not a matter of either/or, it is a matter of both/and. Thriving churches will yoke the two oxen of prayer, the here and now and the then and there, into a team pulling a spiritual load together. This then is a call for balance. A balance between the legitimate prayers for the temporal and the imperative prayers for the eternal.

Thriving churches, while praying for legitimate temporal matters, will focus much of their prayer power on issues of eternity. Thriving churches will be as passionate over people headed to hell as they are over people headed to the hospital. Recognizing that no amount of nifty programs or ultramodern approaches to ministry can replace the power of the Holy Spirit present to change lives, thriving churches will bathe their every function in prayer not only for God's blessing but also with a genuine burden for the salvation of the lost. It will be found that those churches where intercessory prayers for salvation are heard will also be praying for people from their fellowship to be called as laborers for the harvest. One of the very specific commands in the New Testament concerning prayer is that we would pray that the Lord of the harvest would send forth laborers into the harvest. More on this topic occurs in a later chapter.

> *Thriving churches will be as passionate over people headed to hell as they are over people headed to the hospital.*

I recall from my elementary school days those first real encounters with a magnifying glass. Quite a marvel to a little boy. It was soon discovered that the ability of the glass to magnify was greatly enhanced if the rays from the sun were caught and focused to a point. A device that was designed to magnify could, when finely focused, start fires or carve initials in wood. Paper fires were easy. Initials framed by a heart and burned into the desk were more difficult but possible. It was a question of patience and determination coupled with a continual finely focused shaft of energized light. It really gave the magnifying glass a power far beyond its own.

Thriving churches will finely focus much of their praying on issues of eternity and will start a few fires in the process. Small ones at first. As patience and determination increase and the intercessory burden of the fellowship keeps the focus finely tuned, the shaft of heavenly light will burn some amazing images into reality. Intercessory prayer for the lost will give a church a power far beyond its own, for one convert is living testimony of a power at work in the fellowship that is far beyond anything of its own creation.

Thriving churches will understand that their mission is to lead people to the cross not to the church. With that priority understood, the focused point of prayer—the wedge of intercession—will be for salvation, not merely for God to somehow bless what we are doing. As an outgrowth of such a thriving prayer priority, both the Kingdom and the church will be built, bringing joy to everyone involved except the devil!

At your next prayer group meeting, suggest that only requests of eternal significance be mentioned. What seems eternal in terms of possible impact to one may not seem so to all. That's okay. The deliberate exercise to focus beyond now to then, beyond here to there is in itself a stretching exercise of real worth. Perhaps a prayer time where the only requests brought forward for the group to consider are the names of unsaved for whom the prayer participants are genuinely concerned. An on-purpose reaching beyond ourselves.

A reading in a contemporary hymnal catches the sense of balance in prayer that will mark thriving believers. It says,

Prayer, mingled with faith, brings salvation to the

sinner, healing to the sick, joy to the sorrowful and hope to the discouraged. It causes the enemy to flee, unlocks the great treasure house of the Lord, opens windows of heaven and brings down showers of blessings upon the humble Christian.

Thriving churches will focus prayers on the issues of eternity. It's not a matter of gifts or talents, location or population base. It's a matter of the heart. *SEIZE THE DAY!*

CHAPTER SEVEN

A THRIVING CHURCH WILL . . .

GIVE MORE TO OTHERS
AND SPEND LESS ON ITSELF

THE AVERAGE CHURCH IN AMERICA ALLOCATES ABOUT FIVE PERCENT OF ITS BUDGET FOR EVANGELISM, BUT APPROXIMATELY THIRTY PERCENT FOR BUILDINGS AND MAINTENANCE.[22]

—GEORGE BARNA

THE MISUSE OF MONEY BLOCKS MORE MINISTRY IN THE LOCAL CHURCH THAN ANY OTHER SINGLE CAUSE.[23]

—PAUL ROBBINS

"Share with God's people who are in need"
Romans 12:13.

The scene is all too familiar. The TV preacher is begging for money. Immediate help must come or the "ministry" will go out of business. Belly up. The appeals are heard so often from so many corners as to have become both wearisome and suspect. The excesses and impropriety of some of these individuals have cast a heavy veil of distrust on nearly all TV preachers who are presumed guilty by association. There are quality ministries dedicated to Christian principles and bona fide needs exist in some cases, no doubt. Too often, however, it seems that the viewing public is being asked to financially bail out the unwise decisions of high profile preachers.

> *It takes more than a slick appeal to produce a sustained money flow to support ministry. A slick appeal can produce a short burst, but it takes something more for the long pull. It requires integrity.*

The high pressure appeals have become so routine as to cause some Christians to flip to another channel or to turn off the TV when the preachers start their predictable "we must have your help" monologue. Give-aways and guilt trips are a part of many of these appeals. And the money is not coming in. Many reports verify huge reductions in income for a long list of TV ministries. It takes more than a slick appeal to produce a sustained money flow to support ministry. A slick appeal can produce a short burst, but it takes something more for the long pull. It requires integrity.

The contrast is so stárk as to be startling. He operated orphanages in England. Hundreds of children literally were dependent on him for their very lives, their food and shelter. Lacking governmental or institutional underwriting of his budget, George Mueller carried an awesome fiscal and spiritual burden for those in his care. We are told that when Mueller needed to raise money, as he so often did, he went to God in prayer, not to the people for money. He and those working with him believed that people could be moved by prayer alone which meant that no pledges were signed, no financial pleas expressed. And the money arrived. Not just once. Over and over. Repeatedly, God's people responded just in time with just enough. No slick appeals. No give-aways. No emotional twists and guilt trips. Prayer.

Money and ministry. A necessary union. A frequent point of misunderstanding and tension. Is it appropriate to ask for financial support for ministry? Is it appropriate not to ask for financial support for ministry? Should we only pray? Do we even need to pray about such matters or just follow the known biblical principles of stewardship? Where is the line between faith and foolishness when going into debt? Should we have debt at all? Is it sinful or spiritual or neither to maintain a large balance in the church's treasury? Should everybody be expected to tithe? Should anybody be expected to tithe? Money and ministry.

> *Money and ministry. A necessary union. A frequent point of misunderstanding and tension.*

There are various traits related to money that often mark the philosophy of a surviving church. None of these, when isolated by itself, is harmful or negative. In fact, there is value in some of the attitudes that drive these traits. But taken as a group, these characteristics reflect either a fortress mentality that has more trust in the balance sheet than in God or a reckless abandon of fiscal responsibility growing out of a twisted view of stewardship and a cavalier presumption on God.

Included in this less than exhaustive list are the following:

1.   ACCUMULATE AS MUCH MONEY AS POSSIBLE.

This trait reasons that we must maintain a strong and growing balance on hand in our general fund since you just never know when we might need the money. This trait takes a principle of responsible stewardship to an extreme extension and drifts into a hoarding attitude and is proud of it. The focus is on gathering rather than giving.

2.   DON'T EVER ACCUMULATE ANY MONEY.

This flip side trait from number one above assumes the equally unbalanced view that to have any money on hand is to be placing trust in ourselves and not the Master. Therefore, all monies must be drained out by month's end. It's spiritual to do so, it is reasoned. This is one of the traits of "Theophobia," a fixation with God that renders people so heavenly minded that they're no earthly good! The focus is radical rather than reasonable.

3. GET OUT OF DEBT AND STAY OUT OF DEBT.

This trait would have us believe that we just can't support another ministry or missionary and certainly cannot consider adding staff or building more facilities because we are making double mortgage payments now. This view sees paying off the mortgage as the number one priority of the church. Attempts to fulfill the Great Commission are delayed or canceled in the headlong drive to burn the mortgage. Tunnel vision sets in and the church moves along and like a horse with blinders on fails to see the broad picture due to its self-imposed narrow field of vision. The freeing of the church from long-term debt becomes the misdirected purpose for existence. The focus is on means rather than ends.

4. GO DEEPLY IN DEBT AND TRUST GOD.

Another flip side trait that is so unstable as to be unable to stand when held up to the light of faith and reason. The followers of this piece of nonsense advocate "trusting God" for all financial matters and almost question the spirituality of anyone who suggests that the principles of fiscal responsibility were intended to apply to the body of Christ. Such attitudes, when in control, have led more than one church into a survival mode with its oppressive atmosphere of paralyzed existence under a debt load impossible to carry and the church staggered or perhaps even collapsed. The focus is on a twisted view of faith that denies facts rather than a healthy view that balances faith and facts.

5.   ASSUME FINANCIAL OBLIGATIONS ONLY IF CASH AND PLEDGES ARE IN HAND TO COVER THE TOTAL COST.

Pushed too far, this overly conservative position renders God unnecessary. If no obligation is accepted until funds are on hand or promised, then there is no faith exercised at all, except in the people to meet their promises. No growth or stretching is necessary, just hold the fort and collect the committed money. The focus is on us not Him.

6.   BOARD MEETINGS CONSUMED WITH FISCAL CONSIDERATIONS.

This trait exhibits itself in the fine-toothed review of the treasurer's report with questions and discussions followed by questions and discussions while Great Commission matters get little attention or are forwarded to the next meeting due to lack of time. Bean-counter mentality dominates the meeting and makes the treasurer's report THE item of the agenda. Scratched nearly to death by this fine-toothed comb, the meeting trickles to a conclusion and matters of eternity are kept on the back burner. The focus is on the scaffolding rather than on the structure.

7.   BOARD MEETINGS THAT VIRTUALLY IGNORE FISCAL CONSIDERATIONS.

This flip side trait is a twin to number four above. It reasons that the time necessary for a financial statement is a needless intrusion into time that could better be spent pursuing dreams for the ministry of the church. The bean-counters have been replaced by the pie-in-the-skyers who are equally lethal to a true vision for ministry. Excesses or bad decisions or sloppy fiscal habits are overlooked as some grand plan for tomorrow is refined while denying the truth of today. It's the ostrich syndrome—the old head in the sand routine that fools no one except the ostrich. The focus is blinded rather than balanced.

8.   HOW MUCH WILL IT COST?

This trait shows up as the first question asked when any new ministry or idea is advanced for discussion, always weighing the value of any new concept by dollar impact rather than divine inspiration. It's not that the question should not be asked.   It must come forward as new ministries are considered and existing ministries evaluated.   In surviving churches, this question comes early in the discussion.   Not by design but as a reflex response that reflects the mentality of the fellowship. The focus is on cost not value.

9.   WHAT'S IN IT FOR OUR CHURCH?

If we agree that we can swing the cost, how will it help us? This trait is a close second place follow-up to the how-much-will-it-cost question when examining new ministries or re-evaluating existing programs, always focusing on internal benefit not ministry to others. This narrow view examines ministries from a selfish perspective. It takes the admirable desire to build the local church and carries it to an unhealthy conclusion that the only items worthy of support are those that help us. It misses the outward thrust dimension of balanced ministry. The focus is on us not them.

We must be responsible stewards of the resources God has placed in our hands and under our control. This is no call for a disregard of fiscal management and responsible stewardship. It is a call to move away from the stifling and strangling habit of many churches to evaluate every opportunity for ministry in terms of dollars needed. This is a call for balance.

The bills must be paid. Salaries must be met. Mortgage payments must be current. Our witness and perhaps even our existence are at stake. But these things are not the issues, the philosophy of ministry is the issue.

Thriving churches will responsibly care for their fiscal obligations but will also spend generous sums of money on others in this dynamic decade. The fiscal thinking of such churches will exhibit various traits as illustrated in this less than exhaustive list.

1. TRUST GOD'S CONTINUING LEADERSHIP, NOT THE BALANCE IN THE GENERAL FUND, FOR THE FUTURE.

    This trait, while recognizing the need for fiscal common sense, relies on the Master not the money. Decisions are cast in a context that recognizes that a true faith venture commits us to the current challenge only after it has been bathed in prayer and withstood the safety gained by the counsel of the many. This does not render the known fiscal strength of the church irrelevant. It is an integral part of the decision-making but not the final determining factor. The "divine intervention follows human effort" principle is in full bloom here. Under God, we do our best and trust God for His continuing intervention as we pursue Great Commission ministry to the best of our collective ability. The balanced focus is on Him and us.

    They built a functional new church in a city where I pastored. It stretched them but in a healthy manner. A challenge, not a millstone around their neck. The pastor was once asked who would help pay for the building. With realistic faith he responded that people who did not presently even know that the church existed would be won to Christ through their ministry and they would be discipled and would help to carry the financial load. It turned out to be just that way. Faith balanced with divine direction.

2. THE OBJECTIVE IS TO BE OUT OF BONDAGE NOT
    NECESSARILY OUT OF DEBT.

    This trait acknowledges that a responsible level
    of debt is almost always a part of the reality of a
    thriving church but the debt level is never
    allowed to reach suffocating proportions. There
    are those churches alluded to earlier that strangle
    in a fiscal soup they cooked themselves. There
    are others obsessed with burn-the-mortgage-
    fever. The thriving church will avoid both of
    these extremes.

    The cycle that replaces a retired mortgage with a
    new commitment has often marked the history of
    growing churches. That cycle will continue to be
    in evidence in thriving churches. Often funded
    by a relatively short-term stewardship campaign
    in the church rather than long-term conventional
    debt, thriving churches will continue to expand
    and offer need-driven ministry. The load will
    always be noticed but never crippling. It will
    require the fellowship to stretch but never to
    snap. Balance.

3. BOARD MEETINGS HEAR FINANCIAL REPORTS BUT
    DWELL ON GREAT COMMISSION ISSUES.

    This trait recognizes the need for good and
    accurate financial reports but centers discussion
    on broad Kingdom issues not nickle and dime
    stuff. We must always have adequate reports.
    No suggestion is being advanced for slipshod
    approaches to money management and reporting.

Just perspective. Money is a ministry tool. It is not the center of ministry. The bottom line must be known. How the church got there must be understood. Where the church is going fiscally must be clear. In thriving churches, however, board or trustee meetings do not spend an excessive amount of time spinning their wheels in the rut of fiscal mud. The big picture is kept in view.

4. NEW MINISTRY POSSIBILITIES ARE EXAMINED WITH A GREAT COMMISSION CONSCIENCE NOT A COST-EFFECTIVENESS APPROACH.

This trait evaluates new ministry concepts according to their perceived ability to do good in the name of the Master. Financial implications and costs are necessary but secondary discussion items.

5. HOW WILL IT HELP OTHERS?

This trait evidences the biblical truth that it is more blessed to give than to receive. The outward focused ministry must not be allowed to jeopardize the local base to the point of threatening its financial life. Neither must such ministry be undertaken only when it is perceived as helping just our little bunch. Money must be invested in real ministry not just spent for programs to amuse ourselves. Thriving churches will once again strike a balance.

6.   ARE OTHERS ALREADY DOING THIS EFFECTIVELY?

This operative question will lead some thriving churches not to undertake certain ministries. No church can do everything well. In some cases, if others are already providing effective ministry in some specialized area, thriving churches may decide not to launch a competing ministry at all. Good use of money does not warrant endless duplication of ministry in a spirit of competition. Kingdom building is a driving motive for thriving church decisions on program dollar expenditures.

The fiscal management philosophies just discussed will enable thriving churches to live and breathe in an atmosphere of positive challenge. Because the major dollar commitments of such churches are balanced and appropriate, they will be both willing and able to respond to a variety of crushing needs both across town and around the world. Some surviving churches will be held captive by their financial decisions and as a result will be willing but unable to respond to needs outside their church but in the family of faith.

Thriving churches will support missionary enterprises outside North America. They will send work teams with both skilled labor and blank checks. They will support church planting. They will share in local ministry to the homeless, the transient and others in immediate crises. Fiscal management will make frontline ministry possible.

He came to a conference in Swaziland where I was serving as chairman. Through an interpreter he asked that I express appreciation to the American church for the used clothing that had been sent. Without it, he said, the delegation from Mozambique of which he was a part could not have been present. Their country was ravaged by civil war and the clothes from America made a very real difference. Reflecting on how little it had cost us in America to provide discarded clothing to a people to whom it obviously meant so much was at the same time rewarding and convicting.

> *Fiscal management will make frontline ministry possible.*

Thriving churches will give more to others and spend less on themselves. It's not a matter of gifts or talents, location or population base. It's a matter of the heart. SEIZE THE DAY!

CHAPTER EIGHT

A THRIVING CHURCH WILL . . .

HOLD ITS CHILDREN LOOSELY AND CELEBRATE WHEN THEY ARE CALLED INTO FULL-TIME MINISTRY

THE BIBLE KNOWS NOTHING OF VOLUNTEERS, ONLY THE CALLED.[24]

—GORDON MACDONALD

"Be careful to do what is right" Romans 12:17.

If called to be a minister, don't stoop to be a king
. . . so goes the oft quoted verbal missile of a leader of
the past. But times have changed.

In many contemporary churches and church
families, it seems that the focus of celebration is pointed
towards the young people who excel academically and
as a result pursue careers in medicine, law, engineering,
computer science and the like. The anticipated salary
and benefits packages combined with the prestige of
these professions makes them attractive to both
graduating high school seniors and their parents. While
these are all good and noble pursuits, this is a call for a
return to the romance of a call to vocational ministry.

And then there is our outsized fixation with sports.
A doctor or lawyer is one thing. A professional sports
hero is the real thing. Fame and fortune. Such
opportunities will come to very few persons overall and
when they do occur close to us, they warrant a real
celebration no doubt. But this is a call for a return to the
romance of a call to vocational ministry.

This is not suggesting that the "uncalled" should
volunteer for the ministry. I knew a young man who
claimed a call to vocational ministry, prepared himself
academically for ministry and accepted a small pastoral
charge. After one or two rather unspectacular years, he
resigned his church and withdrew from the ministry as a
profession. When asked why he was making such a
dramatic change he stated that he entered the ministry in
the first place only because his mother thought it was a
good idea. Bad idea. As pointedly stated earlier, the
Bible is a chronicle of the ministry of the called, not a
volume of the exploits of volunteers. Not the driven.

Not the volunteers. The called. Called by God. The inner awareness that I can do no other.

> This is not suggesting that the "uncalled" should volunteer for the ministry.

This is not an attempt to make the vocational minister appear more dedicated or holy than others. This is not intended to convey that minister types—preacher creatures—are the only ones following God's plan and all others are somehow on a secondary track. God's will for all of us is to be in ministry in the broadest sense of the word. For all Christians, ministry is an avocation. For some however, it is a lifetime, full-time vocation.

While no desire exists and no attempt is made to minimize the value or worth of any profession, this is a call to celebrate with and about those persons whom God will call to full-time ministry. The thriving church will rejoice when its finest young men and women enter the ranks of the vocational ministry. There will be no sense in the church and hopefully in the family that a call to ministry is unfortunate or beneath the skill level of the individual or somehow a secondary use of the talents and gifts of the person called.

Our materialistic society has made its inroads into church thinking at more than one point. This is one of those insidious places where our values have been warped a little and a subtle attitudinal shift has taken place. More than one person who felt a call to ministry also felt an underlying current of cold water being thrown on their plans amidst the "how nice" speeches of some of the saints. Occasionally, the water is thrown straight at the exposed heart of the newly called person.

I was called to ministry while still in high school. Following graduation, I decided that I preferred to be rich rather than righteous and for several years pursued a career in business. Awareness of the call on my life never faded. Some seven or eight years later after a real spiritual struggle and after seeking counsel from one I trusted totally, I surrendered to preach, resigned my job and prepared to return to college. My wife and I stored our furniture, moved in with her parents who lived nearby so that my wife could keep her job while I went away to college. Quite an adjustment. Many in our church and in our families offered encouragement and support. But then there was the cold water. And from an unexpected source at that.

> *If God calls you, watch out for the cold water, often from the unexpected. Take an umbrella and keep on keeping on!*

My wife and I went to pick up a few groceries one day during this time. In the store we met an individual from our church who wanted to know why I was leaving a promising business career to enter the ministry. God didn't need people of business promise quitting their jobs to chase off after the ministry. Keep your job, make lots of money and give heavily to the church was the counsel offered to me. Talk about cold water. I shivered inside from the effects of the drop in temperature this individual caused. But it did not dampen the reality of the fire that God had placed within. If God calls you, watch out for the cold water, often from the unexpected. Take an umbrella and keep on keeping on!

Not just young men and women will be called from thriving churches. While this is and perhaps will always be the dominant model, it is by no means the only pattern the Master follows. There is a growing trend toward mature individuals moving into vocational ministry while in their 30s and 40s and beyond. A most successful pastor friend of mine went to seminary when he was 35 years of age and is now pastoring a vibrant and growing church. Just a few days ago, I was asked to be involved in counseling with a man who is now 46 years old and is sensing a pull to ministry. It was my privilege to ordain together a man and wife who are both hovering around the 60 birthday mark. I recently took part in a service where a man, 81 years old, was being commissioned as a minister. It was a moving time to share with him in what, by his own testimony, was a high-water mark of his four score and more years. A bit unusual no doubt. But in thriving churches, God will place His hand for vocational ministry on people across all spectrums and the church will celebrate. God will not be limited in His moving by our stereotypical concept of the ideal minister.

If you should sense God's stirring in your spirit, please avoid the error of limiting the Master by thinking that God could not use you in ministry for whatever reason may be presently invading your mind. Spend time in prayer, in the Word and seek competent counsel as you proceed in your search. If the stirring you feel is God at work, it will intensify, and good advice from trusted Christians will confirm the direction the Spirit seems to be leading.

Surviving churches want to hold onto their best people. In fact, sometimes surviving churches will whine when someone from the faithful group is called to ministry. Their outreach thrust is dysfunctional to the extent that they have little hope of replacing the one leaving for ministry preparation. They want to keep all their people at almost any cost. After all, it slows the downward spiral of the fellowship. Tunnel vision whines. Kingdom vision celebrates. Tunnel vision is bitter. Kingdom vision is bittersweet.

> *God will not be limited in His moving by our stereotypical concept of the ideal minister.*

Thriving churches, while sensing keenly their loss, celebrate when their best are called by the Master to full-time ministry. No suggestion is offered here that a thriving church should be of such unrealistically lofty stripe that no regret is felt at losing top-notch people from the fellowship. Only the dead would not be affected by the departure of the near and dear. Thriving churches rise above their sense of personal loss because a broader vision is in place. Building the Kingdom is the focus, not just building the church.

He was convinced that God was calling him to lead his church to mother another fellowship a few miles away. As an outgrowth of this pastor's world-class philosophy on Kingdom building, the church planting pastor was encouraged to visit any and all of the people of the mother church with the purpose of inviting them to be a part of the new daughter church. The pastor of the mother church publicly stated his goal and desire to see 100 of their best people become a part of the daughter church.

When the daughter church was born, some 80+

persons from the mother church became a permanent part of the new fellowship. The mother church pastor had made the birth of the daughter possible and virtually assured its success by "giving away" these key persons. Incidentally, the mother church grew by more than 300 in attendance during the next year and the daughter reached an average attendance of about 500 in the same 12 months.

While the issue was not the calling of persons into full-time ministry, the philosophy and attitude of the pastor and people made it a celebration when some of their best left for another ministry. Thriving churches will celebrate in this same manner when some of their best are called into full-time ministry.

A vital part of the ministry of a thriving church is to lead its people to focus on eternity and not on retirement, to consider the afterlife, not only the good life. While projected salary and benefit packages may drive many vocational decisions, the driving force for the called out ones is the God-given determination to do the very best to the very last. To go, as He calls, with a message of salvation and Spirit-filled living, of hope and healing to the last, the lost, the least and the lonely. To go reflecting the thrust of the quote from Admiral Yamamoto of the Imperial Japanese Navy who, when he was planning the attack on Pearl Harbor said, "Our objective is maximum damage to the enemy not minimum risk to ourselves."[25]

The pastoral role model in thriving churches will enhance the calling of ministers and missionaries. The pastor's love for, commitment to, and fulfillment from ministry will be evident. There will be a spirit of servanthood and perhaps even sacrifice that stands in stark contrast to the materialistic infection raging in

America. Those whom God might be calling will be able to observe a role model conducive to the Spirit's moving. It might be successfully argued that some ministers have seen few persons called to the ministry under their ministry because their own role model held up a less than inspirational and fulfilled example. Conversely, it might be successfully argued that some churches have seen few persons called to the ministry from their ranks because their attitude toward and treatment of pastors has been such that the model cast was not conducive to pastoral recruitment.

It has been said by some who have studied in detail the calling of persons into ministry that only about 10 percent of all persons called receive an instantaneous call. For about 90 percent of persons the call is a process with many tiny streams of inner impulse, circumstance and events leading to a river of awareness that "woe is me if I preach not the gospel." It may well begin with an inner restlessness, a tug at the edges of the heart. The inner impulses will be confirmed by the Word of God and further validated by the trend of circumstances. These three ingredients in sequence are strong indicators of divine direction. However the call comes, thriving churches will celebrate such movings of the Master in their fellowship.

The parental support given by thriving Christians will be positive and will celebrate when sons and daughters are called to ministry. There will be no flak fired at the fledgling prophet by outwardly pious but inwardly selfish parents. In thriving churches, parents will have received world-class teaching and will rejoice when their children are touched by the Master for ministry. It was a great asset whose value cannot be calculated for my wife and me to both have parents who not only celebrated our call to ministry, they also sacrificed to help us follow through on that call. They threw a prayer blanket over us, as it were, and did all that could be hoped for and more as the call was followed and fulfilled. World-class parents for certain.

Thriving churches will celebrate the calling of its people into full-time ministry. It's not a matter of gifts or talents, location or population base. It's a matter of the heart. *SEIZE THE DAY!*

CHAPTER NINE

A Thriving Church Will . . .

INTENSELY SEEK THE SALVATION OF THE LOST

WE LIVE IN THE MIDST OF A VERY FERTILE LAND, BUT EVEN A FERTILE LAND HAS TO BE PLOWED, SOWED, AND CARED FOR BEFORE IT WILL PRODUCE A CROP.[26]

—DONALD MCGAVRAN

EVEN THOUGH MOST CHURCH PEOPLE BELIEVE THAT THOSE OUTSIDE CHRIST ARE LOST, MANY FAIL TO MOVE BEYOND THAT POINT.[27]

—MICHAEL HAMILTON

"Never be lacking in zeal" Romans 12:11.

"The majority of our pastors are practicing Universalists," he said. Startling. In a meeting where I was present this statement was made by a highly ranked officer of one of America's largest denominations. A denomination whose grand history was forged on the anvil of the gospel message preached with power in earlier generations. He then followed up by advising us that the great need of his denomination was for pastors who would again believe the Bible. It seems incredulous that such a statement could be both advanced and accepted as truth. With purpose and determination we evangelicals declare that this could never happen to us. That's what the generation that preceded him in his church said also.

While those of us generally identified as evangelicals may not suffer from a lack of New Testament vision to that extent, a creeping sense of universalism is quietly invading the church. The songs that spoke of a passion for souls and that plead with the Lord for a vision for the lost seem gone, not only from the hymnody of the church but perhaps from her very psyche as well. It is not that some major heresy has invaded. It is not that the faith of the fathers has been abandoned. It is not that the absolute necessity of salvation has escaped our thinking. Priorities have subtly shifted.

How long since you have heard or preached a sermon on judgment or hell? Not an angry vindictive diatribe but a thoughtful and compassionate handling of these biblical truths. The horrifying prospect that our own family members and friends could be eternally separated from Christ seems to be clouded in our minds.

It's as if we believe that somehow they will get in at the last. That creeping universalism mentioned earlier. Going to church has become a more vital priority than coming to Christ. The concept of sinners in the hands of an angry God is largely lacking from our thought patterns.

> *Going to church has become a more vital priority than coming to Christ.*

In many circles the thrust of evangelism is on accepting Christ and rarely on conviction of and sorrow for sin. It is almost as if we do Christ a favor by accepting Him into our hearts. This leads to the erroneous extension of thought that says if I do not accept Christ then He is somehow disadvantaged rather than the grim reality that I am damned. For years, the evangelical movement overemphasized the cost of refusing to serve Christ. Hellfire and damnation sermons were common. Some claimed you could almost smell the smoke and feel the heat. The heavy weight of the message centered on the stark reality of spending eternity separated from God. Very little preaching focused on the benefits to the believer but rather on the costs to the nonbeliever. It was the hard sell approach. Out of balance.

We have quite successfully corrected that over-emphasis. Preaching now largely centers on the benefits of grace in the believer's heart. The God-can-help-you-be-better sermons are everywhere. The thrust of this style of contemporary preaching rightly aims at maximizing our potential for His glory. Truly a noble objective. The quest for effective and acceptable ministry to the baby boomers and baby busters has also nudged preaching even deeper into the equipping mode. There is almost no suggestion that there are eternal consequences for failure to serve Christ. Not culturally acceptable some would tell us. Little or no focus on costs to nonbelievers. Almost total thrust on benefits to believers. It is the soft sell approach. Out of balance.

In many evangelical churches, an entire year or more may go by without a single new convert coming to Christ and few of the members seem disquieted. In fact, many members may not even realize this sad state of affairs exists. In some churches the justifiable need for discipleship has so captured our energies that there is virtually no thrust toward the salvation of the lost and little or no deep heart concern over the matter. Donald McGavran once said,

> The greatest obstacle to the growth of the church is the belief in splendid church work, whether the church grows or not. In America today, many Christians are interested solely in perfecting existing Christians and not in finding the lost and discipling them.[28]

Why are such statements about the contemporary church able to be made with accuracy? Many reasons. A few are listed.

1. FLATTENED VISION

    The admonition is to lift up our eyes to the harvest. More often than we are comfortable admitting, the vision drops and centers on the various issues in the local church. Sometimes negative. Fights, misunderstandings and petty bickering. Sometimes positive. New disciple-ship classes. The building program. It is possible to look in two directions at once, both up and around. At least in our spirits. Up to the harvest. Around us to the challenges of vital ministry to the body.

Naturalists tell us that the eagle has two focusing points in its vision pattern. It is able to see in a normal depth perception manner and also has a second set of lenses that can be called into use that act like binoculars to zoom up a distant object for a closer look. Thriving churches will have two vision points. One up to the harvest. One around to the must-do tasks of ministry.

2.   FATTENED SOCIETY

We are called to minister in a society that feels little need for God. Hardship stirs the soul and plenty puts it to sleep. Recessionary cycles in the economy take a bite out of us once in a while but basically the North American people are living in the lap of luxury in comparison to much of the rest of the world. Such living creates a sense of self-importance and self-sufficiency that renders God unnecessary except in case of emergency. Nice thoughts about Him at Christmas and Easter but that's about it.

> *Thriving churches will be sensitive to societal needs, bends and trends but will also with compassionate clarity declare all the counsels of God.*

In such an environment, preaching or ministry that suggests that all is not well and that more than we can provide for our families is terribly necessary in the long run is not popular. Not popular but necessary. "When they shall say peace and safety . . ." Thriving churches will be sensitive to societal needs, bends and trends but will also with compassionate clarity declare all the counsels of God.

3.   FALTERING PRAYER FOCUS

This was covered in an earlier chapter. One of the reasons for the de-emphasis on evangelism in many churches is that we have neglected to pray for a burden for the lost as well as for the lost themselves. Passion for the sinner has surrendered to prayers for the sick. Broad-based prayers will be among the marks of a thriving church.

4.   FINANCIAL PRESSURES

Some churches and the people in them are not carrying a burden for the lost because they are staggering under a burden of debt. So much worry is focused on paying the mortgage that the good news has been relegated to the outer provinces. Thriving churches will keep the big picture in view.

5. FRACTURED RELATIONSHIPS

Evangelism grinds to a halt when Christians are involved in attacks on each other. When we are deeply and emotionally involved in internal conflict, our effectiveness at touching others with the gospel is neutralized.

6. FAULTY CHURCH GROWTH ATTITUDE

This attitude makes the growth of our local church the number one priority of all that we do. It tends to weaken the demands of the biblical message on the one hand and to rejoice over trouble in First Church down the street that might help us out a little on the other hand.

7. FORSAKE THE VITAL IN PURSUIT OF THE VALUABLE

There is a proliferation of religious groups around today. There is a strong nondiscrimination movement afoot in the society. Put these two together and the message of salvation can be eclipsed. The rationale goes like this. To suggest that a person's religion is not the true faith and that ours is the real thing is discriminatory. Therefore, the reasoning goes, no one should suggest that their belief is "right." The vital is sometimes submerged by the valuable. The vital message is driven under the surface by the valuable—good interfaith nondiscriminatory relationships.

I was in a community some time ago where there had been internal unrest in more than one church over power struggle issues and related carnal matters. As a result, people transferred membership and attendance around among four different evangelical churches. The net result was that one church "grew," one church "held its own" and two churches "lost." In reality, nothing happened. Kingdom population was the same size as before all the fussing. The apparent "growth" was only a mirage. No one was converted. No sinner was redeemed. In fact, the message may have been weakened due to the community's knowledge that the churches were engaged in low-level internal war.

Transfer growth merely builds some local church at the expense of another. Conversion growth builds the Kingdom. Obviously, there are many times when transferring to a Bible-believing church is both appropriate and necessary, but growth by conversion should be, must be our first passion.

In surviving churches, rejoicing is heard over one brother or sister who transfers from the sister evangelical church down the street. Sometimes rejoicing is heard because, bless God, we held our own and didn't lose any to the sister church down the street. I believe the devil and his bunch also rejoice over such out of focus priorities.

In thriving churches, rejoicing is heard over sinners that repent. With open arms of fellowship transferring members are welcomed, but real celebration is focused on sinners coming to the Christ. Whether in the public services of the church or in their own homes or in the pastor's office, thriving churches see the lost redeemed.

> *A sense of the need to build the Kingdom surpasses the sense of need to build the church.*

In thriving churches the climate for effective evangelism is present. The expectation that people will be saved as a result of the ministry is very strong. A sense of the need to build the Kingdom surpasses the sense of need to build the church.

How is this attitude built? How does this spirit develop? There are many possibilities. A few are listed here drawn from the Sunday school choruses of yesterday:

1. *One door and only one and yet its sides are two; inside and outside on which side are you?*

    This is a matter of categories. In the first community where I pastored there was a small 30-bed hospital. On one occasion, there were two men in adjoining rooms who were both dying with cancer. One was a millionaire senator. The other was a common laborer. In the light of the realities of eternity facing both of them, there was only one distinction that mattered. Which side of the door they were on.

    I was asked to preach in my home church one Sunday early in my college preparation for ministry. A frightening experience. The pastor, sensing my uneasiness, offered a brief prayer prior to our going out on the platform. He said, "Dear Lord, help this young man to understand that every face into which he looks this morning is going to heaven or hell. Amen." I already knew that. He was not imparting new knowledge. He was bringing the truly important into perspective. *One door and only one.*

2. *The wise man built his house upon the rock and the foolish man built his house upon the sand. And the rains came down and the floods came up and the house on the rock stood firm and the house on the sand fell flat!*

This is a matter of foundations. Not long ago I was in a church that was celebrating its 100th anniversary. Various pastors of the past were sharing events remembered by them. One man told of coming to the church many years ago when the congregation was very small and the building in a poor state of repair. One day the floor of the sanctuary actually dropped about a foot to the ground below because the foundation gave way.

Our passion for the salvation of the lost will be sharpened when we resist the cultural tendency to admire superstructures and consider anew God's requirements for foundations. In 1 Corinthians 3:11 we read, *"For no other foundation can anyone lay than that which is laid, which is Jesus Christ."* A life built on anything other than

Christ is built on sand. No exceptions.

3. *My desire, to be like Jesus, my desire, to be like Him. His Spirit fill me, His love o'erwhelm me. In deed and word to be like Him.*

This is a matter of priorities. A resharpened perspective on the reality of categories and foundations is quite likely to cause a realignment of our priorities. What is truly important again becomes important. The redemption of the lost takes on new urgency.

4. *This little light of mine, I'm gonna let it shine. Let it shine, let it shine, let it shine.*

This is a matter of purpose. An intentional premeditated decision to represent the Master among the multitudes. Not burn people with the flame or hide it under a bushel. Neither of these extremes. A steady light shining forth in a dark environment. A balanced witness.

5. *I will make you fishers of men if you follow Me.*

This is a matter of Jesus' promise. He continues to use human instruments as His agents to those in need of forgiveness.

These five items are simply a restatement of the known. An observation of the obvious. However, a renewed and intentional focus on the absolutes of categories, foundations, and His promise coupled with appropriate priorities and purpose on our part are attitudinal and mind-set matters vital to a sharpened vision for the unsaved.

Thriving churches will refuse to be satisfied with only biological and transfer growth. Thankful but not satisfied. Such churches will maintain a high profile on both the need for and the results from sharing the message of redemption.

Thriving churches will intensely seek the salvation of the lost. It's not a matter of gifts or talents, location or population base. It's a matter of the heart. *SEIZE THE DAY!*

CHAPTER TEN

A THRIVING CHURCH WILL . . .

JOYFULLY WORSHIP, SERVE, AND SACRIFICE — A BIT RADICAL!

IN THE WEST, SECULARISM HAS AGGRES-SIVELY SPREAD IRRELIGION, TURNING EUROPE INTO A POST-CHRISTIAN CULTURE AND AMERICA INTO A BATTLEGROUND WITH ORTHODOX RELI-GION IN RETREAT.[29]

—CHARLES COLSON

I WILL TAKE NO BACKWARD STEP.[30]

—U. S. GRANT

"Be joyful . . . " Romans 12:12a.

Methods alone, even correct methods, will not produce a New Testament church. The mechanics of proper procedure must be accompanied by the dynamics of apostolic power.

We can neither work up nor shout down such workings of the Spirit in our midst. Apostolic power is not a commodity to be purchased down at the local Christian bookstore. It cannot be stored in the custodian's closet for our use upon demand. A surplus from some great high experience cannot be held over to draw on during some dry day. A sovereign God moves among His people as He chooses and not when or where we timidly suggest or dogmatically demand. I do suggest, however, that a climate conducive for such movings of the Master among us is created when we joyfully worship, serve and even sacrifice.

There are those who worship and serve primarily out of a sense of duty. Duty is a high and noble motivation and our entire society would better function, no doubt, if the general populace understood and did its duty. In fact, a strong case could be advanced that many churches would function at a higher level than present experience if the key people in the fellowship understood and performed their duty as a part of the body of believers. In Acts 23:1 we read, "Then Paul looked straight at the Sanhedrin and said, 'My brothers, I have fulfilled my duty to God in all good conscience to this day.'"

In surviving churches, the dominant motivation for service will be centered in duty. Sermons will often deal with a variety of "you should do better and give more and be more faithful in attendance" themes.

Negative motivation will be utilized and people will too often be recruited for worship attendance and service in the church from a guilt trip or pressured selling approach.

Good people will serve in such settings and will in many cases do their very best to assist in the programs of the church. And good will be accomplished. But fatigue will set in early. Service only from duty tends quickly to burn out. Frequent staff turnover and constant recruitment just to staff-existing programs are among the marks of the duty-driven church.

There has been a tendency in many evangelical churches to place available people in empty positions with little or no attempt to match gifts and needs. This has occurred with disturbing frequency in the filling of pulpits as well as with the staffing of volunteer positions filled by lay persons. Such a short-sighted approach has resulted in frequent turnover and high frustration level on all sides. In the late stages of these mismatched assignments just before the volunteer becomes exasperated and quits, duty becomes about the only active factor in the "hang in there" days near the end.

My son was enrolled in a first-grade class in a Christian school that had a good reputation for offering a solid values-based educational experience. The teacher assigned to his class was an experienced and qualified educator with many years experience. Her many years experience, however, was in teaching twelfth-grade math. A mismatch. The students were not rebellious or learning-disabled. The teacher was not incompetent or disinterested. Her commitment and dedication were obvious. The problem was that her gifts and training did not match the needs of the hour. Frustration set in. The situation deteriorated. Changes were made under some emotional stress. Not a happy life chapter. All because of a mismatch.

In a thriving church, duty for service is yoked with joy in service and that combination yields willing and fulfilled workers. Sermons will often deal with "God has made a difference in your life and you can make a difference in the world" themes. Positive motivation will be utilized seeking to match the needs of a position of service with the gifts and talents of those available to serve. Those who serve will do so out of a heart that truly desires to be of service to Christ and the church.

Good people will serve in such settings and good will be accomplished. Leadership will highlight the high value of such ministry to the body. Service will not necessarily be for a lifetime and sabbaticals from service will be celebrated. There has been an all too common tendency of people to fear that if they agree to accept a ministry assignment in the church it means a life sentence without parole. Specific short-term assignments and the understood expectation of regular relief from intensive service will quiet that fear. Burnout will be infrequent and people will serve out of a sense that combines "I want to" and "I must," not merely from an "I must" attitude.

There are those who will look on such joyful expression of duty and accuse us of being a bit radical. I welcome such comments. In more than ten years in church administration I have never once been called to a church to restrain the radicals and freeze out the fanatics. More than once I have been called upon to referee scuffles over minor, almost ridiculous, issues.

To be considered a bit radical in our service to the Master is a powerful compliment. Not radical in lunatic fringe belief patterns. Not radical in pursuit of some emotional black hole. Not radical in legalistic demands of behavior or dress. Radical, as the world measures values, in our willing service to the Lord Christ. This is not a call for the toxic kind of involvement that goes far beyond reason in its addiction to activity in the name of commitment in ministry. Neither is this an endorsement of the "sit back and watch and let others do it because I'm too busy to be involved" attitude. This is a call for balance. Not an obsession to activity and not an observer of activity. Balance. Focused, balanced, and joyful service to Christ through the ministry opportunities in our local churches may cause us to appear a bit radical, however.

In a society where the care and feeding of "number one" has become the primary motivation for many people, those who joyfully serve others stand in rather sharp contrast. It looks a bit radical. A case could be made that the average church is so subnormal by New Testament standards that if it ever got back to being normal it would appear to many to be abnormal.

This is a call for balance. Not an obsession to activity and not an observer of activity. Balance.

In a thriving church, duty for service is yoked with joy in service and that combination yields willing and fulfilled workers. Sermons will often deal with "God has made a difference in your life and you can make a difference in the world" themes. Positive motivation will be utilized seeking to match the needs of a position of service with the gifts and talents of those available to serve. Those who serve will do so out of a heart that truly desires to be of service to Christ and the church.

His generation clearly saw Him and His followers as radicals. They were on one occasion referred to as those who had turned the world upside down. Our fathers in the Protestant movement were considered radicals at least and often heretics. Our freedom in the faith was purchased in part with the blood of martyrs whom the world thought were a bit radical.

No case is being made for doctrinal oddities in the name of progress and enlightened thinking. No case is being made for extremism in the name of Great Commission fulfillment. The truth is, however, that thriving churches will be peopled with those whose level of joyful service to Christ will be such a sharp contrast to the "Sunday morning Christian" syndrome as to appear a bit radical.

That edge of joy will cut into worship as well until it too will be marked by warm expressions of joy in music, fellowship and pulpit ministry. In some settings the music may consist of worship choruses sung to the quiet accompaniment of a guitar and in other settings may consist of the grand old hymns of the church sung to the majestic accompaniment of a pipe organ. It is not the style of music or worship form that will primarily determine joy in worship. It's a matter of the heart. It's spirit and attitude and vibrancy in Christ that sets the tone. In thriving churches, worship is an experience to be enjoyed, not an exercise to be endured. In thriving churches the people will hear a message from God, not a sermon from the office. In thriving churches during worship people will look at the Christ. In surviving churches during worship people will look at the clock.

Vitality is the characteristic in focus. Not the promotion of emotion for its own sake. Not the suffocating of emotion in order to overcorrect some excess. Emotion drives happiness while vitality drives joy. It is joy that the thrivers will exhibit. Emotions reflect the present circumstances. Joy reflects the presence of Christ.

> *In thriving churches, worship is an experience to be enjoyed, not an exercise to be endured.*

Thriving churches will also exhibit to the world the paradoxical characteristic of joyful sacrifice. In addition to the privilege of regular financial support to the local church, thrivers will give additionally of their time and money to worthy projects. Such giving will sometimes even brush against the sacrificial.

He pastored a church in a large southern city. Several young people representing a parachurch group came to his door one Sunday afternoon. Conducting a one-question survey they told him. He agreed to cooperate. They then asked my friend what sacrifices he had made for Christ since becoming a believer. A stabbing question by his own testimony, he stood in awkward silence for a few moments and then informed the inquirers that he had made no sacrifices. A few inconveniences perhaps. No sacrifice.

The concept of sacrifice is foreign to modern-day affluence-driven thought patterns. Stewardship is a real hurdle and sacrifice seems totally impossible to some and quite unnecessary to others.

As you might have supposed, this is a call for balance. This is no appeal for an extreme view of sacrifice that espouses the disposal of all possessions, the distribution to the needy of the revenue gained thereby, and the retreat into the unreal world of presuming upon God to meet needs we created ourselves. Nor is this an endorsement of the "gather and grab" mentality so dominant in our culture.

Sacrifice as understood and practiced by thrivers is not some negative idea designed to impoverish the reluctant. It is a very positive concept and practice. True sacrifice is the giving up of one thing for the sake of another of higher value.

His name was Eric Liddell. His story is well known to many and was effectively told in *Chariots of Fire*. A missionary to China. A devoted Christian. Died in captivity in a Japanese concentration camp during World War II. He was also an athlete. A short-distance runner with the 100-yard dash as his best event.

> *True sacrifice is the giving up of one thing for the sake of another of higher value.*

He was selected to represent Great Britain in the 1924 Olympics in Paris, France. He agreed to compete so long as he did not have to run on Sunday. When the schedule of the events was released, the 100-yard dash was to be held on Sunday. He told his coach he would not run. The pressure mounted on him to shift his position this once.

As the pressure continued to build, the Prince of Wales, later to be King Edward VIII, asked him to compromise his position. He was sacrificing a strong possibility of earning a gold medal, he was told by His Highness. World fame. Glory for the home team and the British empire. Eric refused to bow to the prince or the pressure.

Another runner came forward and agreed to switch events with Liddell. As a result, Eric Liddell competed on Tuesday in the 400-yard race and won the gold medal for the British. He stood on the center dais and as "God Save the King" played in the background, and the Union Jack fluttered in the breeze, the gold was placed around his neck. No compromise. The world on Sunday thought he was a radical unreasonable zealot. On Tuesday, they thought he was an exonerated hero. But the world has never truly understood the dynamics of sacrifice.

The issue here is not Sunday sports or Sunday observance. Those are only illustrations of the point in this case. True sacrifice is the issue in focus. Sacrifice is the giving up of one thing for the sake of another of higher value. To Eric Liddell, the "sacrifice" of a seemingly sure gold medal on Sunday was for the higher value of remaining true to his own personal convictions of right and wrong. Many thought he was a bit radical. Crazy even. The world cannot cope with those whose deep commitment to the higher value spills out in their behavior patterns.

Thrivers will sacrifice in this same type of context. Giving up those things that some of the world counts of great value in order to be true to personal convictions of right and wrong. Surviving churches will admire such sacrifice. Thriving churches will have in them those who model sacrifice. The giving up of something the world thinks of value for the sake of another thing that the other world knows is of higher value.

It may be money. It may be a promising career to pursue a call from God to vocational ministry. It may be vacation time in order to serve on a short-term missions trip. It may be postponing the purchase of a new car to assist in the work of the Kingdom. It may be the surrender of dreams for our children as God calls them to some ministry. The higher value is the focal point.

Thriving churches will joyfully worship, serve and sacrifice. It's not a matter of gifts or talents, location or population base. It's a matter of the heart. *SEIZE THE DAY!*

CHAPTER ELEVEN

A Thriving Church Will . . .

KEEP A LOCK ON THE BACK DOOR

As Americans grow increasingly hardened and skeptical, the built-in credibility of Christianity will be steadily reduced in people's minds. Christians must communicate the importance of the faith by exhibiting a lifestyle based upon a Christian philosophy of life.[31]

—George Barna

Gandhi is reported to have said that he might have become a believer if it hadn't been for the Christians.[32]

—Vance Havner

"Be devoted to one another in brotherly love"
Romans 12:10.

He went as the new pastor to an old hidebound church. Within the first year he reported that he undertook a membership drive and drove out fifty. Out the back door that is. His action was deliberately aimed at culling the crowd. It was a "shape up or ship out" kind of operation.

There are times in the life cycle of a church when such overt weeding action may be warranted or even required. The health of the body sometimes requires the surgical removal of unhealthy parts. In the exercise of appropriate discipline in the family of faith there are those occasions when the back door needs to be opened wide and some folk "invited" to exit. Occasionally, not often. Never as a first response and only as a last resort. A healthy church has a back door but its hinges are rusty from infrequent use.

He pastored a church that I had occasion to visit about every six months or so. The church was growing and many new people were being touched by the ministry in that place. The average attendance of the congregation never grew by a number even close to the number of new people coming into the fellowship. Every year or so it seemed as if the congregation was almost entirely a turnover except for a solid core in the center. The hinges on the back door were warm from their more or less constant use. In truth, the rapid people movement left the impression that the church was a revolving door. In the front door with excitement and in a very short loop, out the back door of disillusionment or misunderstanding.

The potential for a great church was there. It was

never realized, however, because the church specialized in obstetrics and neglected pediatrics. The fellowship was very effective at seeing people won to Christ but the new babes were left to starve to death in the delivery room. There was no deliberate decision to neglect the newborn. Their great need for care and feeding was simply not recognized or believed to be of importance. It was assumed that somehow they would grow and mature unassisted. The dynamic of the Sunday services and early work assignments in the church were seen as the almost exclusive tools in the pediatric department. It was like feeding beef steak and giving a bicycle to a newborn. A few made it. Many died and drifted out the back door.

Surviving churches will have a back door that is either worn from regular use or seized shut from no use. Some will see new people come into the church rather often but will fail to stem the tide out the back door and after much activity, not much progress is realized. Those who leave are blamed for not being spiritual or dedicated or serious in their search for a maturing faith. A survival mentality in the church can never accept that the church itself might need a little help in pediatrics. It is always their fault. The attitude exuded says that we have the truth and they just won't line up. Occasionally true, but often this attitude reflects a self-imposed tunnel vision that is purposefully blinded to the broad picture. In this Helen Keller axiom mode, the back door hinges are kept oiled by those who don't even realize they are on the oil can team.

Conversely, there are those surviving churches whose back door is seized shut because no new people have entered the front door in so long that a stifling routine has set in. The group is reduced to the "I shall not be moved" bunch and the back door is not a problem.

In churches that truly thrive, there will be an active front door and a largely inactive back door. A large percentage of those who visit will revisit and a large percentage of those who revisit will be assimilated into the church. The back door will be locked. These churches will face real obstacles in their assimilation processes. In the book *Mastering Outreach and Evangelism* the authors identified ten such obstacles. They are large family networks; existing friendships; facilities; a church's history; special events; philosophy of ministry; a reputation of tension; confusing service styles; class and cultural distinctions; poor attitudes.[33]

How is a church to overcome these obstacles, many of which are unavoidable? While there are programmatic responses to this question, there is much that can be accomplished in keeping the back door locked that comes from the heart. Assimilation is not entirely driven by dollars or programs. While these things are necessary, the most vital traits of effective assimilation come from the heart, not the pocketbook or program booklet. Consider the following vital traits of the heart that lead to effective assimilation.

ATMOSPHERIC PRESSURE

The atmospheric pressure readings on the barometer indicate what is happening with the weather patterns. When the pressure is rising, the weather will improve and when the pressure is falling, conditions will worsen.

My wife and I were involved in special services in a small rural church one time. A visitor came in one evening and with his family took a seat in the center of the church. In a few minutes, one of the pillars of the assembly came in and observed the visitors in "his" seat. He asked them to move. There were plenty of other seats but he asked them to move. Unbelievable. Sad but true. They moved all right. They left and I did not much blame them. They found the back door before the service ever began.

> *Atmosphere is perhaps the single most crucial factor in the response of the first-time visitor.*

If you could have talked with the pillar after that event, you would have discovered that he really loved the Lord and would have loudly proclaimed that he wanted the church to grow. And I believe he did. He worked for the back door company and did not even realize it. Some would say he had no sense. He certainly had no sense of atmospheric pressure. It dropped through the floor right in the midst of his blissful ignorance.

Thriving churches exert a lot of effort on atmosphere. Atmosphere is perhaps the single most crucial factor in the response of the first-time visitor. If the first-timer never returns, the back door was found the first Sunday. Atmosphere is a major contributor to the answer of the "will we go back again" question. Atmosphere, where?

*Parking lot. Is there adequate space for the visitor to find a place to park without circling the parking lot in increasing frustration? Do the faithful take the best spaces themselves up close to the church or leave those for the searchers? If it is raining or snowing, are there parking lot attendants ready with an umbrella to assist the visitor to the building? Are spaces designated for the handicapped and are those designations honored? If the lot is crowded and spaces limited, are there traffic directors to assist in the finding-a-spot process? Atmosphere builders.

*Lobby. Are there greeters who greet? Are the other people mingling in the lobby who are not the assigned greeters warm and friendly or do they represent a cold front passing through? Are clear directions provided so the first-timer does not suffer a temperature spike trying to find out what to do next? Is there an indication where the washrooms are located? Do the greeters transition the visitor to an usher who can assist in seating? Do the greeters use mouthwash? Atmosphere builders.

*Nursery. Do the nursery attendants look like the kind of people you would want to leave your baby with if you were a stranger? Is the nursery clean and well lighted? How does it smell? How is it decorated? What is the baby-to-worker ratio? Is the staff pleasant? Atmosphere builders.

*Ushers. Do they consult with the visitor about seating options? Do they usher to a seat rather than just point with an "have at it" attitude? If the congregation is already singing, does the usher provide a hymnal open to the appropriate page? Are the ushers identified so the visitor knows the person invading their space is a properly designated helper? Do the ushers also use mouthwash? Atmosphere builders.

All of this occurs before the first-timer has even heard word one from the preacher creature. The atmospheric pressure of the visitor has established a reading by this point that will dramatically affect the remainder of that visit and the yet-to-be-made decision of whether to visit again.

Then there is the worship atmosphere itself. Music styles and worship forms will vary and no one style or form is within the comfort zone of all people. Some will like our style and some will like their style. On a first visit, there is one thing that influences the atmosphere for the visitor more than style of music or worship form, more than the sermon content or delivery, more than the length of the service or the personality of the preacher. This primary atmosphere influencer is whether or not the visitor was singled out in any overt way and embarrassed. Many well-intentioned ministers have dropped the atmospheric pressure of a first-timer into the storm zone by embarrassing the visitor in the name of a "friendly welcome." Atmospheric pressure moves people toward or away from the back door. We can control this.

ACCEPTANCE POWER

If the fear of embarrassment is a point of genuine concern with the first-timer, then the fear of rejection looms like an iceberg in the path of the repeat visitor in search of a church home. What color do you have to be to be welcome here? Do you all dress the same? Is this church only for the middle class and above? Are you expected to have background in this denomination? Can I be accepted here is the driving concern.

It is a great church in the making. Located in a large and vibrant Canadian city, it is a multinational and multicultural church. I have been there on various occasions and observed persons of eight or ten cultural and racial groups worshiping together. An inspiring sight. The marvelous diversity of dress reflects cultural background. The multiracial worship team reflects the realities of the congregation. The common thread is a relationship with the Master. No rejection here. Acceptance.

Surviving churches tend to be exclusive. Thriving churches tend to be inclusive. But what about the principle of the homogeneous unit? Don't we all tend to herd together with our own kind? Yes, but thriving churches and surviving churches have different definitions of "our own kind." To the survivors, our own kind refers, in large measure, to socioeconomic status, race, and culture. While thrivers are aware of all these common bonds, our own kind refers to a higher issue and that is membership in the family of faith. That does not negate the issues of status, race or culture but it holds these matters against the tapestry of Calvary love where distinctions of status, race and culture tend to fade and blur. Acceptance. It keeps people away from the back door. We can control this.

AUTHENTIC PRODUCT

Atmospheric pressure—no embarrassment. Acceptance power—no rejection. Authentic product—no deception.

It is the belief and behavior matter. It was the problem for Gandhi. He might have become a believer if it were not for the Christians. Their beliefs were acceptable. Their behavior was not. Deception.

The new people who begin to identify with our churches are looking for many things and among them is an authentic faith and genuine followers of that faith. Kids and new people share a common characteristic.

They can smell phonies. We surely have seen our share in the church world the last few years. The litany of the fallen reads like a bad horror script. It is a deep tragedy that some "Christian" leaders have been living in hidden immorality for years or have been convicted of criminal activity or have made repeated journeys into the land of the lowlifes. In some cases, the tragedy has been exacerbated by the failure of the guilty to admit guilt and seek forgiveness. We need to understand, we are told.

> *Surviving churches tend to be exclusive. Thriving churches tend to be inclusive.*

In the process of all this, the credibility of all believers has lost ground. When searchers come to our church, they must find that we live an authentic life. Integrity. No deception. It goes a long way toward keeping the back door locked. We can do this.

ADEQUATE PROGRAMS

Thriving churches will have adequate programs both in the church and on the computer. One to train and the other to track.

This is where the pediatrics matter comes into focus. The new babies in the family of faith must be nurtured and hand-fed in the early days of their new life. Discipleship was discussed in an earlier chapter and will not be revisited in any detail here. Such things as a "Welcome to the Family Class" or a "New Converts Class" and making midweek contact are corporate attempts at pediatrics. One-on-one discipleship is a higher level of pediatric speciality vital to the growth of the baby. Thriving churches will have adequate programs of ministry at this life-or-death touch point. Effective discipleship is a real back door slammer.

> *The possibilities are limited only by our vision.*

Technology also plays a part in keeping the back door closed. Our computers can and must be harnessed to, among other things, identify newcomers; maintain a newcomers directory; keep the new babies informed of opportunities for fellowship and family interaction; accumulate and store vital data on the family for touch points at special times throughout the year. The possibilities are limited only by our vision. The right programs at church and on the computer can further contribute to a closed door at the back. We can do this.

The back door. Always there. Never totally closed. Too often swings wide because well-intentioned people unknowingly use an oil can on the hinges rather than a lock on the door. Thriving churches will place great emphasis on the lock. Thriving churches will see the back door open only infrequently. Keep a lock on the back door. It's not a matter of gifts or talents, location or population base. It's a matter of the heart. *SEIZE THE DAY!*

CHAPTER TWELVE

A THRIVING CHURCH WILL . . .

LIVE AND BREATHE AN UNSWERVING COMMITMENT TO EXCELLENCE

I WANT TO MANAGE THE CHURCH TO GOD'S GLORY. ANYTHING LESS CONTRADICTS THE CREATOR, WHO AFTER CREATION SURVEYED HIS WORK AND SAID, "IT IS GOOD." HE DID NOT SAY, "OH, IT'LL DO."[34]

—DON COUSINS

COMMITMENT TO EXCELLENCE TAPS AN INCREDIBLE SOURCE OF ENERGY.[35]

—ROBERT SCHULLER

"If it is possible, as far as it depends on you, live at peace with everyone" Romans 12:18.

". . . try to excel in gifts that build up the church" 1 Corinthians 14:12.

People are unreasonable, illogical, and self-centered. Love them anyway.

If you do good, people will accuse you of selfish ulterior motives. Do good anyway.

If you are successful, you will win false friends and true enemies. Succeed anyway.

Honesty and frankness make you vulnerable. Be honest and frank anyway.

The good you do today may be forgotten tomorrow. Do good anyway.

The biggest people with the biggest ideas can be shot down by the smallest people with the smallest minds. Think big anyway.

People favor underdogs, but follow only top dogs. Fight for some underdogs anyway.

What you spent years building may be destroyed overnight. Build anyway.

Give the world the best you have and you may get kicked in the teeth. Give it the best you've got anyway.

Excellence strives to live on the high road and is guided by standards like these. Mediocrity settles for the low road or for in-between on the misty flats where the rest drift to and fro.

Many good people have found the wheels of their lives mired in the misty flats of mediocrity. Given the absolute reality of gravitational pull, all things fall freely and are raised to higher levels only by deliberate and determined effort. All things will fall on their own. Nothing rises on its own. On this playing field, good people often drop to the misty flats by force of nature and not by purposeful decision.

Mediocrity is one of our enemy's most insidious weapons. It does not entice the believer to withdraw from the fellowship. It does not entice the believer into open sin. It just draws the Christian off the high ground onto the misty flats. Impact for God and good is largely neutralized when one is a flat dweller.

Mediocre is defined by Webster as "of middle quality, neither very good or very bad; ordinary; average; commonplace." This characteristic has invaded much of the thought processes and philosophies of life of our current generation. We have become conditioned to expect and accept less than the best.

> *Thriving churches will be marked by a pursuit of excellence. Surviving churches will be marked by a defense of the mediocre.*

A Canadian manufacturer of electronic devices entered into a supply contract with a Japanese maker of subassemblies, specifying a five percent defect rate, according to the company's usual purchasing practices. Sure enough, exactly five percent of the subassemblies that began arriving were defective. Conveniently, the defective devices were packaged separately from the good ones, and were labeled as such.

Astonished, the Canadian purchasing manager inquired about this anomaly, and was informed by the Japanese agent that his company was happy to supply the defectives but had wondered why the Canadians wanted them in the first place. Mediocrity has so gripped our culture that we expect and accept defects, even plan for them. We do not even seem upset by it and therein lies the real danger.

> *Thriving churches will reach toward the stars. Surviving churches will reflect on their scars.*

No call is being made here for an unreachable absolute perfection or for a smothering perfectionism. This is an appeal to do our very best until the very last and while recognizing that we cannot always excel we will never be satisfied on the misty flats. Thrivers will with constant purpose and great effort seek to lift our ministry onto an ever higher plane.

Thriving churches will be marked by a pursuit of excellence. Surviving churches will be marked by a defense of the mediocre.

Thriving churches will reach toward the stars. Surviving churches will reflect on their scars.

Thrivers ask, What can I do for the church? Survivors ask, What can the church do for me?

Thriving churches offer to God what is best. Surviving churches offer to God what is left.

Thriving churches attempt to excel. Surviving churches attempt to explain.

In his book *The Pursuit of Excellence* Ted Engstrom says,

> As you observe those who excel, be on the lookout for specific qualities that set them apart:

a. Personal discipline
b. Vision
c. Optimism
d. A sense of adventure
e. Courage
f. Humility
g. Humor
h. Confidence
i. Anger
j. Patience
k. Integrity[36]

> *Thrivers ask, What can I do for the church?*
> *Survivors ask, What can the church do for*
> *me?*

As stated at the outset, this book is focused toward mind-set and heart-set. Excellence fits so naturally into such a thrust. A commitment to excellence is within the volitional grasp of every one of us. No exceptions. Our level of performance and list of accomplishments will vary widely, often determined by factors beyond our control. I sincerely believe that our greatest gift to God is to rise to our highest potential for His glory. A purposeful commitment to excellence is the starting point for such a life goal.

Excellence is a matter of spirit. It grows from the heart and filters into the very fiber of our life until a reputation for doing it right emerges. But it begins that journey in the heart. A matter of spirit. Consider these ten references to spirit and their impact on our unswerving commitment to be the best we can be for His glory.

1.   HASTY SPIRIT. "He that is slow to wrath is of great understanding: but he that is hasty of spirit exalteth folly" (Prov. 14:29 KJV).

A man entered a drug store and asked the druggist for something for the hiccups. The druggist, without saying a word, reached across the counter and slapped the customer right across the mouth. The customer shook his head and said again that he wanted something for the hiccups. "Well, you don't have 'em now do you?" asked the druggist. "Never did," replied the customer, "the medicine was for the wife out in the car."

A hasty spirit reacts without all the facts. It acts on assumptions and misunderstandings. It shoots first and asks questions while picking up the bodies. It is impulsive and quick-tempered. It is the way of the mediocre.

2.   HAUGHTY SPIRIT. "Pride goes before destruction, and a haughty spirit before a fall" (Prov. 16:18 NKJV).

This is the look-what-we-did bunch. We had 500 Sunday—how many did you have? Quite impressed with themselves and their accomplishments. Tend to dominate discussion whenever possible with self-talk and inward focused praise. Obnoxious. These types remind one of Mrs. Olsen on *Little House on the Prairie*. The only person who thinks highly of her is herself. They are Babel Syndrome folk. They said, "We really are something." God said, "Is that so?" It is the way of the mediocre.

3.   HELPLESS SPIRIT. "Whoever has no rule over his own spirit is like a city broken down, without walls" (Prov. 25:28 NIV).

Walls were the primary and first-line defense against the enemies of the land. Without walls, the city had no defense and was helpless before the opposing army. The enemy had easy and immediate access.

This is different from the hasty spirit discussed earlier in both time line and intensity. Hasty spirit is the first-shot hotshot. Helpless spirit keeps at it out of a grim determination to win the battle even if it means losing the war in the process. Not in a rage, just not in control. The walls are down. It is the way of the mediocre.

4.   HURT SPIRIT. "A man's spirit sustains him in sickness, but a crushed spirit who can bear?" (Prov. 18:14 NIV).

Our reaction to a hurt that crushes will call both our best and worst selves to the front. The rain falls on the just and the unjust and the storms crash into the lives of the mediocre and the excellent. No one should be expected to enjoy or not be crushed by devastating hurt. The dividing line between excellence and mediocrity is not the level of devastation. Rather, it is in the spirit manifested in the midst of the devastation.

As one of a past generation observed, a container of honey cannot spill one drop of vinegar no matter how suddenly bumped. There is no suggestion that we should enjoy the spill, only a question of what comes out when the container is tipped over. It reveals our spirit, whether high road or misty flats or perhaps even low road.

5. HUMBLE SPIRIT. "The Lord is near to those who have a broken heart, and saves such as have a contrite spirit" (Ps. 34:18 NKJV).

Submission. A concept understood by both the excellent and the mediocre. Practiced by the high heart and resisted by the flat dweller. I mean submission to the Master and to properly constituted authority. Not toxic submission to self-appointed dictators and strutting little kings presiding over kingdoms of their own construction.

In the "me" culture around us, submission is a tough pill to swallow. It is a biblical principle that comes to bear directly on the lives of believers. This is not a doormat concept. This is not a depreciation of our uniqueness as one of God's creations. This is a teachable spirit concept. This is a listen and learn spirit. This is a spirit that approaches the Master saying I am so glad to be in Your presence rather than a "You should be so glad I took the time to come into Your presence" spirit. It is the way of excellence.

6.   HONORABLE SPIRIT. "A talebearer reveals secrets, but he who is of a faithful spirit conceals a matter" (Prov. 11:13 NKJV).

Did you hear? Three highly toxic and unhealthy words in the mouth of the mediocre. The flat dwellers focus on the sensational and the items that reflect negatively on another. Gossip-mongers. They mistakenly believe that they can lift themselves up by tearing down others. There are some folk around the church who are more reliable in spreading news around than CNN. If you want it told, tell them. If you want it told quickly, tell them it is a secret. There are even some pastors who glean their preaching illustrations from private counseling sessions. It is the way of the mediocre.

Did you hear? Three body-building words in the mouth of the excellent. The high-roaders focus on the uplifting, the encouraging, and the God-honoring. They can keep a secret. They can be trusted. They can avoid the urge to share in every willing ear the unsavory and seamy.

A little boy was being pressured by a friend to reveal a secret he had agreed not to tell. Finally, after much pressure from his friend, the lad with the information said, "Can you keep a secret?" Thinking he had finally worn him down, the second boy quickly responded, "Yes!" "So can I," said the boy with the information and walked off. It is the way of excellence.

7.   HOPEFUL SPIRIT. "I call to remembrance my song in the night; I meditate within my heart, and my spirit makes diligent search" (Ps. 77:6 NKJV).

There has got to be a way out. A song around the church some years ago said, in part, "Anyone can sing when the sun's shining bright, but you can have a song in your heart at night." The mediocre sing in the sunshine and pout in the dark. The excellent sing in the sun and sing in the dark. It may be a different song, but a song nonetheless. The mediocre suck their thumbs. The excellent sing a song.

Paul and Silas sang at midnight in the jail at Philippi. The jailor was converted. On that missionary journey, the first converts in Europe came to Christ. In time, the Europeans brought the gospel to America and in turn the Americans have taken the gospel literally around the world. Quite an outcome to that missionary journey. Quite a song in the night. It is the way of excellence.

8.   HOLY SPIRIT. "Create in me a clean heart, O God; and renew a right spirit within me" (Ps. 51:10 KJV).

This is not talking about THE Holy Spirit but rather a spirit that is holy. The backdrop setting of the Psalm is well known. King David is caught in the sin cycle involving Bathsheba, Uriah, Joab, Nathan and the later uprising under Absalom. The plaintive prayer was driven by conviction over heinous sins. Lust-Adultery-Murder-Deception-Rebellion. Truly a low-road journey.

A spirit that is holy is often in danger or under assault from issues much less significant than David's mess. About the only redeeming feature of the king's saga here is that when confronted with the truth from God's messenger he did not seek to rationalize his behavior or explain away blame that was clearly his. A right spirit—a spirit that is holy—is more important than our pride that resists seeking forgiveness.

If spiritual failure invades one's life, the mediocre rationalize forever, the excellent request forgiveness. A right spirit within. It is the way of excellence.

9. HARNESSED SPIRIT. "He who is slow to anger is better than the mighty, and he who rules his spirit than he who takes a city" (Prov. 16:32 NKJV).

History has often cheered a man who could take a city. One such person is a man named Norman Schwartzkoff. We all know who he is. Before Operation Desert Storm, few of us knew his name. What made the difference? He took a city. Kuwait City to be exact. We are told that he has been offered a seven-figure book contract, has several movie offers, and receives six-figure honoraria per speech. All for a man who took a city.

In God's economy, one who rules his own spirit is better than one who takes a city. Pretty impressive. That contrast brings a harnessed spirit into the bright light of high-road characteristics. We readily acknowledge our reliance on God's grace active in our lives as vital to our quest to rule our own spirit. It is the way of excellence.

10. HONEST SPIRIT. "Blessed is the man . . . in whose spirit there is no deceit" (Ps. 32:2 NKJV).

This is the integrity issue. Is our word to be trusted? Is our conduct when nobody is watching to be trusted? Is our income tax return to be trusted? Is our resume to be trusted? Is our slant on the controversy to be trusted? Is our statistical report to be trusted? An honest spirit. It is the way of excellence.

Surviving churches will be largely populated with residents from the misty flats. A few may be high-road travellers. The church will be dominated by flat dwellers and will never rise above that cloudy plane on any consistent basis. A few sorties to the high ground perhaps, but then the survivors will settle back to the foggy and familiar confines of the bog.

> *Thriving churches offer to God what is best.*
> *Surviving churches offer to God what is left.*

Thriving churches will be congregations of spirit. While always having those few around who are bound by fog and froth, the many will be people of the clear sky found only on the high ground. The church as an entity will exhibit the spirit characteristics of the way of excellence.

From a Charles Swindoll book I first saw this item that he had borrowed from another:

THE WORLD NEEDS MEN AND WOMEN

who cannot be bought;
whose word is their bond;
who put character above wealth;
who possess opinions and a will;
who are larger than their vocations;
who do not hesitate to take chances;
who will not lose their individuality in a crowd;
who will be honest in small things and in great things;
who will make no compromise with wrong;
whose ambitions are not confined to their own selfish desires;
who will not say they do it because everybody else does it;
who are true to their friends through good report and evil report, in adversity as well as prosperity;
who do not believe that shrewdness, cunning, and hardheartedness are the best qualities for winning success;
who are not ashamed or afraid to stand for the truth when it is unpopular;
who can say no with emphasis although all the rest of the world says yes.[37]

> *Thriving churches attempt to excel.*
> *Surviving churches attempt to explain.*

Thriving churches will reflect these traits and characteristics. It is the way of excellence. Thriving churches will live and breathe an unswerving commitment to excellence. It is not a matter of gifts or talents, location or population base. It's a matter of the heart. *SEIZE THE DAY!*

CONCLUSION

Can we take a holy initiative in history? Can we once more strike an apostolic stride? Can we put an ungodly world on the defensive again? Can we show men the folly of opposing Him who has already overcome the world, of rejecting fellowship with the coming King? Will we offer civilization a realistic option, or only a warning of impending doom? Will Christianity speak only to man's fears and frustrations, or will it also fill the vacuums in his heart and crown his longings for life at its best?[38]

In response to these questions from the pen of Carl F. H. Henry, the thriving churches answer *YES*. With God's help, we can and will be a crosscurrent force for God and good in our day and time. We will make a difference.

I once came across an advertising flyer from a political organization urging people to vote. In that document, we were told that:

*   *in 1645 one vote gave Oliver Cromwell control of England.*
*   *in 1649 one vote caused Charles I of England to be executed.*
*   *in 1776 one vote made English the official language of the United States rather than*

> *German.*
> * *in 1839 one vote elected the governor of Massachusetts.*
> * *in 1845 one vote brought Texas into the USA.*
> * *in 1875 one vote changed France from a monarchy to a republic.*
> * *in 1923 one vote gave Adolf Hitler the leadership of the Nazi party.*
> * *in 1941 one vote saved the Selective Service system just 12 weeks before Pearl Harbor.*

In all of these elections or decisions, one person made a difference far beyond anything they could have imagined. He did his part and contributed to the process and unknowingly became a pivot point in history. The ultimate results of his actions far outweighed the seeming insignificance of his individual act of voting.

> *We may not make a difference that rattles history, but we can make a difference.*

There are those whose contribution to the life and ministry of a thriving church will far outweigh the recognized importance of their involvement at the beginning. We may not make a difference that rattles history, but we can make a difference. God may use us as a pivot point to turn a dying or surviving church around a historic corner and into a thriving fellowship. Not because we are seeking to be dramatic or heroic, just because we are doing our best where we are with what we have. Divine intervention follows human effort and as we do our best we openly anticipate His best. We must believe that God can use us to make a difference.

Common people examples are everywhere. She was a widow of limited background and little of the world's goods. She was nearly the only one who still believed the church could prosper there. She refused to quit when the possibilities seemed exhausted. Just a handful. That church now averages nearly 350 in attendance and has had 450 or more on various occasions. Many contributing factors without doubt. One is a little lady, now gone to heaven, who refused to quit in the face of overwhelming odds. She helped make a difference and doesn't even know it.

Average attendance was in the 20s. Two large families and a few others really. They hung tough when it was tough. Many years have come and gone and that church now averages more than 1,100 in attendance and has had a high day of 2,300+. Many contributing factors without doubt. Two of them are the men who headed these two families in that church when they were all there was. They made a difference.

Biblical examples are everywhere. Esther defied the boundaries of culture and went to see the king uninvited. She made a difference. Daniel defied the laws of nature in the lion's den. He made a difference. Moses defied the power of a king in the service of the King. He made a difference. Abraham defied the laws of logic when the son born to him and Sarah in their old age was prepared for sacrifice on the mountain. He made a difference. Paul defied the power of Rome and the plastic religion of the Pharisees. He made a difference.

Church history examples are everywhere. Luther nailed his theses on the cathedral door in protest and his followers were known as protestors and in time protestants. He made a difference. John Wesley took the gospel message out of the confines of the church and to the common man and the Methodist movement was born. He made a difference. Francis Asbury rode on horseback all across the American frontier and left a trail of new Christians and churches behind him. He made a difference. Carey baptized his first convert in India after seven years of labor; Judson won his first disciple in Burma after seven years of labor; Morrison reaped his first new believer in China after seven years of labor. They made a difference. We can make a difference. Probably not a history-impacting difference but a difference nonetheless.

> *Divine intervention follows human effort and as we do our best we openly anticipate His best.*

I do not accept the notion that God has a list in heaven of churches He intends to bless and those He intends to ignore and we are therefore nothing more than passive passengers on the heavenly train. Neither do I accept the notion that we can build great churches whose ministry results will stand the test of eternity so long as our preacher and programs are nifty enough and therefore God's involvement and blessing are nice but not essential. It is not an either/or but rather a both/and proposition. He has already once and for all made an eternal difference. He has left us the privileged responsibility of also making a difference as an agent of the Master among the multitudes.

He was the eyes of the Army of Northern Virginia. A dashing cavalry officer. When J. E. B. Stuart would send communiques to his commanding officer, General Robert E. Lee, he always signed those dispatches with the letters YTCO. I was fascinated to know what YTCO meant and a little research revealed the secret. When Stuart wrote to Lee he always ended by saying "Yours To Count On." As we face the challenges of being a contributing factor in a thriving unit, let us offer to our commanding general a commitment that we are "Yours To Count On."

From Robert Fulghum's fascinating pen comes this account. In closing, let me tell you about Larry Walters.

Walters is a truck driver, 33 years old. He is sitting in a lawn chair in his back yard, wishing he could fly. For as long as he could remember, he wanted to go up. To be able to rise right up in the air and see for a long way. The time, money, education and opportunity to be a pilot were not his. So he spent a lot of summer afternoons sitting in his backyard in his old aluminum lawn chair—the kind with the webbing and rivets. Just like the one you have in your back yard. The next chapter in his story appeared in the media. There's old Larry Walters up in the air over Los Angeles. Flying at last. Really up there. Still in his aluminum lawn chair, but it is hooked onto 45 helium-filled surplus weather balloons. Larry has a parachute on, a CB radio, some peanut butter and jelly sandwiches, and a BB gun to pop some of the balloons to come down. And instead of being just a couple of hundred feet over his neighborhood, he shot up 11,000 feet right through the approach corridor to the LA International Airport. Walters is a practical man. When asked by the press why he did it, he said, "You can't just sit there."[39]

Thriving churches won't just sit there. They will make a difference. It is not a matter of gifts or talents, location or population base. It's a matter of the heart. *SEIZE THE DAY!*

NOTES

[1]James Patterson, *The Day America Told the Truth.* (New York: Prentice-Hall, 1991), pp. 25-26.

[2]Joe S. Ellis, *The Church on Purpose.* (Cincinnati: Standard Publishing Co., 1982), p. 9.

[3]Lyle E. Schaller, *Activating the Passive Church.* (Nashville: Abingdon Press, 1981), p. 35.

[4]Bruce Shelley, *All the Saints Adore Thee.* (Grand Rapids, MI: Daybreak Books, 1988), p. 79.

[5]Paul Borthwick, *How to be a World Class Christian.* (Wheaton, IL: Victor Books, 1991), p. 145.

[6]Leith Anderson, *Dying for Change.* (Minneapolis: Bethany, 1990), p. 119.

[7]Francis A. Schaeffer, *The Great Evangelical Disaster.* (Westchester, IL: Crossway Books, 1984), pp. 29 and 141.

[8]George Barna, *The Frog in the Kettle.* (Ventura, CA: Regal Books, 1990), p. 60.

[9]Charles Swindoll, *Living Above the Level of Mediocrity.* (Waco, TX: Word Books, 1987), p. 163.

[10]Paul Borthwick, *How to be a World Class Christian*, p. 90.

[11]Richard B. Wilke, *And Are We Yet Alive.* (Nashville: Abingdon Press, 1986), p. 40.

[12]Robert Fulghum, *It Was on Fire When I Lay Down on It.* (New York: Villard Books, 1989), pp. 24 and 25.

[13]Warren Bennis, *Why Leaders Can't Lead.* (San Francisco: Josey-Bass Inc., Publishers, 1989), p. 143.

[14]Charles Swindoll, *Improving Your Serve.* (Waco, TX: Word Books, 1981), p. 137.

[15]Ellis, *The Church on Purpose*, p. 63.

[16]Ted W. Engstrom and Robert C. Larson, *Seizing the Torch.* (Ventura, CA: Regal Books, 1988), p. 98.

[17]Larry W. Osborne, *The Unity Factor.* (Waco, TX: Word Publishing, 1989), p. 19.

[18]Robert Fulghum, *All I Really Need to Know I Learned in Kindergarten.* (New York: Villard Books, 1989), pp. 6-7.

[19]Warren Wiersbe, *Victorious Christians.* (Grand Rapids, MI: Baller Book House, 1984), p. 51.

[20]Mario Murillo, *Critical Mass.* (Chatsworth, CA: Anthony Douglas Publishing Co., 1985), p. 26.

[21]Enoch Byrum, *Worship the Lord.* (Anderson, IN: Warner Press, 1989), p. 332.

[22]Barna, *The Frog in the Kettle*, p. 135.

[23]Paul D. Robbins, *When It's Time to Move.* (Waco, TX: Word Books, 1985), p. 113.

[24]Gordon MacDonald, *Ordering Your Private World.* (Nashville, TN: Oliver Nelson, a division of Thomas Nelson, 1985), p. 29.

[25]Gordon W. Prange, *At Dawn we Slept.* (New York: Penguin Books, 1981), p. 203.

[26]Donald A. McGavran and Winfield C. Arn, *How to Grow Your Church.* (Glendale, CA: Regal Books, 1974), pp. 14-15.

[27]Michael Hamilton, *God's Plan for the Church—Growth.* (Springfield, MO: Radiant Books, 1981), p. 15.

[28]McGavran and Arn, *How to Grow Your Church*, pp. 169-170.

[29]Charles Colson, *Kingdoms in Conflict.* (Grand Rapids, MI: Zondervan Books, 1987), p. 113.

[30]Horace Porter, *Campaigning With Grant.* (Alexandria, VA: Time Life Books, 1981), p. 92.

[31]Barna, *The Frog in the Kettle*, p. 126.

[32]Vance Havner, *The Vance Havner Notebook.* (Grand Rapids, MI: Baker Book House, 1989), p. 175.

[33]Frank Tillapaugh and Myron Augsburger et al., *Mastering Outreach and Evangelism.* (Portland, OR: Multnomah Press, 1990), pp. 154-158.

[34]Leith Anderson et al., *Mastering Church Management.* (Portland, OR: Multnomah Press, 1990), p. 17.

[35]Robert H. Schuller, *Tough Times Never Last.* (Nashville: Thomas Nelson Publishers, 1983), p. 177.

[36]Ted W. Engstrom, *The Pursuit of Excellence.* (Grand Rapids, MI: Zondervan Publishing House, 1982), pp. 64-66.

[37]Swindoll, *Improving Your Serve*, pp. 107-108.

[38]Carl F.H. Henry, *Twilight of a Great Civilization.* (Westchester, IL: Crossway Books, 1988), pp. 18-19.

[39]Fulghum, *All I Really Needed to Know*, pp. 139-140.